The Divine Spark

The Divine Spark

Zoltan J. Kokai-Kuun

VANTAGE PRESS
New York

Copyright © 2005 by Zoltan J. Kokai-Kuun

Published by Vantage Press, Inc.
419 Park Ave. South, New York, NY 10016

Manufactured in the United States of America
ISBN: 0-533-15140-6

Library of Congress Catalog Card No.: 2004195721

0 9 8 7 6 5 4 3 2 1

Satirical Reading:

about the source of our existence and about some past great minds, who attempted to explain it, and thereby have helped to shape the future.

This book is full of irreverent thoughts, trying to challenge your own imagination, and your own sense of humor and tolerance.

Contents

Foreword   ix
Introduction   xi

There Is a God

    I. The First Encounter   3
   II. God and Relativity   7
  III. The Nature of It All   13
  IV. Prophets and Pyramids   20
    V. Origin, Identity, Image   26
  VI. T'ai Ki: The Ancient Beginning   34
 VII. The Development of the Cosmos   41
VIII. Brahma—2900 B.C.   46
  IX. Buddha—560–480 B.C.   55
    X. Moses—1250 B.C., or 1450 B.C.,
       or 1590 B.C.   63
  XI. Zarathustra (Zoroaster)—630–550 B.C.   69
 XII. Confucius—550–480 B.C.   73
XIII. Jesus—2 B.C. to 33 A.D.   78
XIV. Mohammed—570–632 A.D.   89

Questions and Answers   99
Closing Words   121
Appendix
   The 21 Points of a 21st-Century Morality Code   125

Foreword

The unprecedented growth of scientific knowledge has been pushing on the doors of ingrained philosophical dogmas for a couple of centuries now. In this book an attempt is made to show how all major dogmatic systems have failed us, and why a new concept of non-religious morality, a new way of thinking should be developed or an old one resurrected and modified to explain the world, logically both within us and outside of us, and make this planet more liveable.

The center of this search, of course, will have to be the nature and the existence of that universal-life-force, which appears to be all round us but has eluded proper, credible definition since the dawn of history. The question is can we do better? The answer is: we should, if we acknowledged and cultivated in ourselves that "divine spark" which must be a part of the universal-life-force, for our lives to have any meaning at all, and therefore, can give us guidance on earth and eventually lead us to reveal the secrets of the cosmos. The journey will be long.

To understand the present, we have to study the past. That is the reason for the historical background of this paper. Yet, I am not striving for great historical accuracy. What I am trying to do is to give an impression of some of history's outstanding, messianic actors in the world's metaphysical theater. In this context I will examine seven religious or quasi-religious thinkers of antiquity to determine the lasting values they have created. Can these values be used and further developed for posterity? Can we, from these values and from the thoughts they inspire, try to put together a "worldview" for twenty-first-century man? Not necessarily without a god, but without religions.

This book is not a scientific inquiry, though it has a deep respect for science. It is a secular inquiry (an intrusion if you like) into a non-secular subject to rekindle the significance of the role of the philosopher, when he tries to answer questions about the nature of the universe. Its aim is to suggest the creation of a partnership between scientific thinking and metaphysical thinking. I would call it a sort of a "free-range" philosophical discussion, to explore how far my speculations can take me in A.D. 2005.

Introduction

Religion is the opium of the masses . . .
. . . and the poison of the soul.

Our origin and place in the universe is an intriguing subject. Many great philosophers, prophets and mystics of the past have tried to build satisfactory theories to explain the beginning of time, the beginning of life, and the formation of the animate essence of man, which we call our soul. They have invariably tied time and existence to the concept of some kind of a spiritual being and appeared to have postulated that the representative of such a spirituality is superior, omnipotent and omniscient in all things.

Eventually, they came to call this representative god, invested him with transparently anthropomorphic characteristics, invented heavenly hierarchies, constructed convoluted religious regimens, and subjected themselves and especially others to these hierarchies, in a continuous power play. Only marginally did they refer to that divine spark in our own makeup, which is indispensable to understanding theories, perceiving things and events around us, creating symbols and concepts, and questioning the nature of life in terms of its relation to itself, to the universe and to a supreme being.

What I have tried to do here is to place this divine spark of man in its proper context; not as a servant of gods, but as a partner in godhood, or at least part of an all-permeating force, which, so far, we can only construe in parables. Do not be shocked by the irreverent questions my ego will ask of this force: if you are looking for hard answers, you have to be tough, even at the risk of damnation, in which, of course, this questioner does not believe. I called this writing a metaphysical satire, because I did not want to create the impression that I am preaching. I also have had the audacity to write it in a polemic form, "a dialogue with god," in which naturally, I have taken the role of god as well. And herein lies the satire of it all. Or perhaps not, because many others have done so before me.

To put this inquiry into proper context, I divided the search into three parts:

1. There is a god.
2. There are no gods.
3. If there are no gods, then what is out there? Is something "out-there" at all; where are we, why are we here, and what is the source of our complex reality?

If you know the answers, then you are already ahead of me.

Part One was perhaps the most difficult, because it had to define the nature of god, the nature of the universe, and the nature of man, in an environment, which cannot be absolute, as the forces, governing the behavior of the basic building blocks of the universe appear to be dualistic. They appear to carry positive and negative charges, which can both attract and repel each other. Therefore, in a relative universe, god must be relative too. This could make it possible for us to communicate with his entity, which we feel should exist, without, however, blind, unconditional adoration, or worship.

In this context, interestingly, the oldest religion, Hinduism, is one of the most tolerant of human frailty and human diversity, despite its severe, caste-conscious social structure. Perhaps this is because Hinduism's deep conviction that the "Dharma," the absolute and eternal cause of the world, has created a pantheon in which, if one god has generated fear in you, you can always turn to another one for solace. The younger a religion is the more intolerant it appears to be, culminating in Muslim fundamentalism. Intolerance is over-compensated fear, and a reaction to insecurity in a psychological void. This is how the universe at first appeared to us. In order to satisfy our craving for security, man's position in his surroundings had to be stabilized. The stabilizing forces in this process were history's gods, whose reality needed reinforcement. Such reinforcement came in the form of strictly formalized, dogmatic religions, which determined not only the code of behavior of the adherents, but the role of gods as well.

It is a characteristic of practically all metaphysical hierarchies that, as a cohesive factor, they have had to rely on fear as far as we mortals are concerned. Yahve is a despot, the Christian God is to be feared, Allah is merciful, but watch out for his prophets!

In this essay I will treat prophets as prophets, spokesmen of some cause or movement; men who used their divine spark to the utmost of their potentials, without any supermanly or special status elevating them above the crowd, and without the claim that they are the only participants in, or representatives of, the universal life force.

Brahma, Buddha, Moses, Zarathustra, Confucius, Jesus, Mohammed as historical persons, or personifications of metaphysical ideas and beliefs, were exceptional human beings but nevertheless, parts of mankind's intellectual evolution. They have no absolute claim to transcendental spirituality, despite their undeniable genius, unless, of course, if you call genius a higher level of spirituality and hypnotic power.

The keyword is "charisma," that extraordinary personal strength, introspective grace, and mesmeric charm, which, when coupled with a superlative ego, can command the attention of the masses. To become a prophet, you have to first believe in yourself. After that, you can believe in god.

Part Two will deal with atheism, in a pseudo framework of

dialectical materialists manner. This is a contradiction in itself, and would muddy the waters, if it could not be traced back to the age-old feeling of mistrust, created by servitude. If taken to extremes, this mistrust will generate hatred against all authorities and lords that be, including the gods and their churches. Reformations and revolutions have started on this basis with varying degrees of success. Of course, such events will not rid the unwashed masses of superstition and fear, and the whole Divine Comedy will start again in a different form. This is because equality does not exist, and the inferior will envy, will be angered by, will hate, and eventually will try to eliminate the superior. Atheism starts with man's desire to compensate for his inferiority. However, not even atheism is absolute, and therefore it will dissolve itself in a new ideological fervor, with new prophets, unless a new morality is found.

Part Three will deal with universes which are only subject to and are only limited by man's imagination. The limits seem to be infinite and, despite their "entertainment-only" character, can be compared to the worlds of science fiction, populated by the extreme creations of futurists. Do we really have cousins out there? This is a fantastically fertile field, which admits inexplicable forces as well, as man-created life-forms, destinies and even demi-gods. Whether this is the composition of the universe, or something in-between, or something quite different, at this moment I only hesitate to think, but respect all thoughts that search into our reality, and bring us a step closer to understanding it. To participate in this search is all I am asking of the reader.

The Divine Spark

There Is a God

I

The First Encounter

To state that there is a god is absurd. To state there is no god is even more absurd. Before we make pronouncements on existence, we should define the nature of the concept. What is existence? What is god? I will tackle these later. First, let us see some arguments.

To say that human beings are the highest form of conscious existence, capable of intelligence in the universe, is probably also nonsense. To postulate that higher intelligences may exist is a very likely, and possibly a valid, supposition. If we start manipulating the relevant symbols which knowledge gives us, we may arrive at the conclusion that we do not understand infinity, yet, having invented a meaning for it, and use for it, we can invent other things as well, such as superior intelligences, such as gods.

We are creative. This is Our Divine Spark.

This is our genius, and this is our problem.

But for the moment let us assume that there is a god, and that this god corresponds to the generally accepted transcendental concepts of "godhood." A superior being, not fully understood yet, but to be revered and worshiped nonetheless. A metaphysical father figure ruling the World, in the stratosphere of universal spirituality.

Having said this, we should stop for a moment, and ask ourselves some questions: Why should we worship? On whose authority? Did he personally communicate with us? Or is he ordering us around through intermediaries? Does he need messengers when he implanted in us his own divine spark which must be capable of "receiving," if we paid attention? Can he oblige us to pay attention or are we only to pay homage? For what? What good has he done for you and me?

By all appearances, he seems to be a cruel joker, who is either experimenting with us in a possibly very scientific way, or playing with us in a most unscientific way. And here lies his vulnerability. He is inconsistent. Unless he does both, in which case he is very consistent and is possibly amused at our simplicity. What is he? What are you lord god? I am asking you to illuminate me about your being, if you are willing. You may just ignore me, or wipe me out for "lèse-majesté," or for blasphemy!

I am still here and waiting. But something is happening! I do not know, if it is only my own thought (probably) or something imprinted on my subconscious brain coming to the surface, but I seem to hear.

What do you think?

I hate it when people answer my question with a question, and almost tell him so, but of course he knows if he is omniscient. But let us not get into that yet. What I think is irrelevant, because it would be only a projection from my memory-bank, with some facetious manipulation of haphazard hypotheses. It is you who has to tell me: are you vulnerable to criticism, or are you above all cosmic and temporal occurrences?

Will you understand it if I told you?

A question again . . . Yes! Because our spiritualities must have something in common, therefore, you can tailor your statement to my "level."

By the way, it just occurred to me, you deserve a compliment! You accepted my audacity, and did not even laugh, yet. God! This is difficult! How can a completely unscrupulous being have ethical considerations as well! Or at least a sense of humor! Of course, these are your mysterious ways. But back to basics: I am listening.

Your question is adequate. You did not ask me if I am good or bad. You asked me about my place in the universe. I could tell you

4

that I am the universe. But even you can understand that the more than hundred billion galaxies, expanding at great speeds, impose some vulnerability on me. I have to expand with them, and that takes a lot of energy. That is the reason that I made the finite part of the universe, where mostly physics rules, to curve: eventually it will return to its own origin, to itself. The infinite part? Your guess is that it is incomprehensible, or perhaps does not even exist? Think about it! I am working on it too.

Heady stuff. Does it mean that you were born simultaneously with the "Big Bang," 13,000,000,000 years ago, separating out as an intelligent super-energy, or a super intelligent energy-complex? Perhaps you did cause the explosion? In cosmic space, whatever that may be, there was this fantastic ball of concentrated, mindless energy bottled up, pressing upon an intelligent nucleus, which could not take it any longer, and blew up the works. The primeval Black Hole has come to life. The Genie in the bottle! It looks as if (and you could almost say) these human tales were based on some cataclysmic events, which somehow have transmitted themselves from matter to mind.

In this context the question is: how does energy differ in the black hole from spirituality, and how does genetic imprintability develop if, due to the "Big Bang," energy races ahead of intellect at the speed of light? Can god catch up? Can god travel faster?

The next possibility is that you are energized space-time itself, and not only supervised the birth of the universe, but planned and induced it as well, staying on the "outside," however, and then calling on the infinitely small building blocks of the cosmos to do your bidding. If these units are recombinant like quicksilver, and omnipresent like an electron, and can obey you, then the number of possibilities is mind-boggling. I find this an interesting theory. If a god can be infinitely small, then it can be everywhere. (And that's what we are told.) If a god can be infinitely small and recombinant, it can be omnipotent, because with something like genetic engineering, it can create the future, or destroy the present. If a god can be infinitely small, it can also be omniscient, because it can ferret its way into the thought process, or any process for that matter. Which one is it?

Neither and all. But do not get discouraged yet! Talking of the universe I tipped my hand to you a little. I did not say:—eventually I will return it into itself—I said: it will return. This means that I gave the universe some basic laws to govern its destiny, fully realizing that it will become accident prone, and that I may have to step in. In this context, indeed, this is a huge experiment, which, however, hardly affects your life span. The other parts of your speculation are so-so. You were closer to the truth, if there is such a thing in your world, when you hinted at a universal spirituality. Perhaps in a thousand generations you might understand that. Next question!

This is encouraging. You plan to keep us going for a thousand generations or so, during which time we can expand our knowledge, the propensity for which we have initially obtained through the "original sin." (This needs an aside!) In Paradise, Eve was audacious enough to pick an apple from the forbidden tree of knowledge, and Adam was stupid enough to bite into it. What would we not do for our women?

By the way: I wonder if the computer system called "Apple" has the pleasure of inspiration from this old story? And did Eve also bite into the apple? And if not: is it from here that male superiority comes? Sacred cows! Do not expect me to be anything other than an iconoclast! I grind my teeth at political correctness, and do not subscribe to either "égalité, fraternité, or liberté," because the bloodthirsty proletarians of the French Revolution left out the most important slogan: justice. This was probably because it did not rhyme with the others. Some say it is implicit. Is it not the other way around? To my mind it is the other three that are implicit in the concept of justice. However, this is a little far-flung from the curvature of the universe, and in any case, you asked me what my next question was?

II
God and Relativity

As universal spirituality will not resolve my day-to-day operation and I am a thousand generations away from solving it, I have to come down to earth to ask about existential reality. Is reality only a perception, is it a theater, or is it an illusion? Tell me about reality, please. Does reality exist, do I have a role in it, or am I only a pawn? My universe is so infinitely small in comparison with yours that my comprehension must be vastly expanded, before I can ask more intelligent questions. Where do I stand?

Naturally, though indirectly, you are one of my creations, but with a proviso: despite my best efforts to make you an unquestioning slave (your Adam concept), I had to equip you with that divine spark, which you came to call your soul, if I wanted to have any kind of dialogue with you. Giving you this infinitesimal equipment, I made you part of the "universal life force," "intelligence," and "spirituality" (you will have to define these terms), and elevated you to the planes of discoveries. This is how you postulated that "I am," or "I am not," and how you were able to observe and analyze the world around you. This way, however, I also gave some of you an insight into my relative limitations and into the contradictions, which this paradox creates. In essence, I endowed you with the ability to think, ask questions and develop concepts. But, before all this, I have diversified you, because I wanted to see where an innate mixture of relatively independent logic and emotions will take you, subject to the color of your skin, or the crook of your nose, or the slant of your eye.

As you hinted at it when you said that I am experimenting with you, my universe is a huge laboratory, and so is yours for that matter, with plenty of potentials for accidents. This means that "the grand design," once it is released, has its own life and its own rules. These rules are not absolute, because absolutes do not tolerate exceptions. Thus, in a non-absolute universe I cannot be either absolutely omnipotent, or absolutely omniscient. However, I can change the course of events, that is interfere with the future, both by evolutionary means and by violent means. It is a moot question whether these conditions impose on me any restrictions that you can perceive. It is also a moot question whether energy existed before me, or I before it, because we both are forces: interactive and inseparable. And where energy exists, there must be polarization. To use a commonplace: that is the nature of the beast. Now, where do you stand in all this?

You are in the middle of my many experiments, which are aimed at transforming energy into matter and into intelligence. As you know, matter can take multiple physical forms, and can also be equipped with the facilities of locomotion and perception in order to acquire intelligence. In this process you have reached a comparatively high level of social and scientific sophistication, interestingly, almost always theocentrical in structure, and almost always based on fear.

It was your basic polarity that created in you a feeling of insecurity, which, in turn, faced with the unknown, made you afraid of your surroundings. By observation you realized that life can be annihilated, including yours, and thereby, your consciousness revoked. You missed the proverbial apple on the tree of eternal life, and you are not really impressed that the only eternity open to you lies in your children. At least for now. And if eternity exists (we can talk about it later), reality exists too, and you correctly perceived yourself and your world (or mine, for that matter) as real. Your role in it? A guinea pig. With some genetic predisposition, and (and you will love this!) with some free will as well! By the way, I have never ordered you to worship me, or even to invent me! You have done a nice job of those yourself, and generously invested me with the idea that I have created you in my image. Nonsense man! I have no image! Actually, I had to start at the sub-atomic level, then progress with amino acids and amoebae, etc., till I arrived at you. (Now you can see the reconciliation between creation and evolution!) In you, I have manufactured something (someone) who can argue with me, and who wants to be like me. Man wants to achieve godhead! Good luck! But don't forget: I am the inconceivable reality. At the moment you are only theorizing about me. It was you who gave me an anthropomorphic supercharacter, you created me in your image, and you have heard that before. But, what you haven't heard is that if I am both energy and intellect, then I either must lack emotions, or must repress them. There is logic in both energy and intellect, and logic does not feel pain or compassion. It took an only partially logical person like you to develop these altruistic concepts and throw them in my face, as if you were telling me something new. I repeat: there is no perfection in the universe. Comets will collide with planets, and man will have to kill to live. It sounds cruel to you, but think about it. Your food-chain is nothing but a series of slaughters.

You will say now that I could have made every living being a vegetarian. Perhaps, but not very likely. The dilemma is that life had to start in water if I wanted to make an early start, or at least water was needed for life, because land was too hot to inhabit. This leads to one of my limitations: fire-resistance is contrary to the character of the process of cellular function which is consumption of nutrients, growth by division, and specialization by imprint. Things had to cool down before mutation became possible. Also, water is the best and most stable solvent to sustain nutrients, which are easily accessible as food to primitive cells which represented life, and required a variety of minerals to sustain their ability to divide and mutate. The more successful mutations, those which happened to encounter the most powerful minerals, soon switched to eating the less successful ones, because they tasted better than minerals. And there you are! The chain has started. The plan is working. I know! I know! You wanted to ask me about the nature of the devil, which is supposed to be a fire-resistant being. Do not forget: the devil is your concept. But as an intellectual counterpoint of my being, it could be explained by your logic. Am I telling you something new?

My god! With one hand you appear to vindicate me somewhat. With the other hand you still puzzle me. And to the devil with the devil.

Let me return to the spark divine, which you so graciously endowed me with, or rather, you endowed your original life-cell, and cultivated it till it evolved into monkeys and humans, proliferating into billions of brain units which will eventually acquire and develop intelligence. I can imagine that you could have supercomputer capabilities, and could keep track of all events and even thoughts, as each unit does have its own calling-card, or wavelength, if you like, but to what end? Out of ten billion units less than 1 percent is creative and contributory to our progress toward godhead! This one percent must represent your favorite "toys," as they are the only ones who can (intelligently), challenge you. To the remaining 99 percent you are still god, anti-god, or no-god, in an absurdity illogical and mind-boggling relationship. There is no evidence that you have not abandoned the 99 percent, to be the pawns of the 1 percent. Yet if we wanted to tell the 99 percent what to do, they will scream blue murder, asking us, "Who do you think you are, God?"

The purposelessness of the whole affair is so blatantly transparent and even irresponsible that one could question why you are still pursuing it, and why we don't see through it and throw in the towel? Actually, that's what we probably are doing, because if this conversation of ours has any meaning at all, then you have betrayed your trust in logic. You have forced emotion on us—which you do not care about—and abandoned the 99 percent, well knowing that you could have eased what we call human suffering, if you wanted to. It looks that the old saying: "absolute power corrupts absolutely" applies to you as well as to us, except on a larger scale, if there is such a thing in a relative universe.

How do you reconcile a policy (so to speak) of non-interference with the mass hysteria of religious adoration? You said, you did not order us to worship you. But people still do. There must be some psychic energy in prayer which penetrates your indifference. How do you handle it?

"Actually," quite easily. I return the task to you. Your mind is a self-contained unit, and with practice, it can control itself. Depending on your temperament (a function of your emotion, which you were complaining about, and which you can also control), you can swear, shrug your shoulders, fly into a rage, kneel down in prayer, or kill yourself. These actions will eventually release your anxieties, and if things turn out right for you, you will thank me, which is not really logical, because it was your own doing. If things turn out badly for you, according to your semantics, you will tell yourself that you were right to rebel, because there is no divine justice or mercy.

If you kill yourself, you are either courageous, or desperate, or a coward, depending on whom you talk to. From my perspective, it is a premature end to one of my experiments. Your energy is absorbed in the universe, and becomes dispersed. No great loss. Not even as much as a pebble in a pond. At least that leaves some nice circles for a while, in which, in a tranquil moment you may find beauty.

There is no beauty in a man's passing, only decomposition. If I interfered, or intervened, the experiment would suffer. You see, your genius is divine in the transcendental sense, and if you used your head instead of your heart you could make that speck of dirt of yours liveable.

This thought-provoking response of yours appears to imply that prayer is not the way to communicate with you; we can dis-

11

cuss things instead, as you did not order us to worship you. Through meditation we can reach you, even if we argued with you.

While on the subject of discussion, however, a remark of yours has struck my ear: you mentioned decomposition as the end of our journey. What happens to our divine spark? If it is dispersed and absorbed in the universal-life-force, as we said earlier, then we can die in peace, because there is no threat on the other side. If you are preserving it for some reason or other then I have to start a new book.

Where do we stand regarding the "immortal soul"?

You will touch on this question later, when you ask me: why should I, your god, recycle old souls when the supply is infinite? Though I could, if it would be logical. And it would only be logical if the experience of all previous lives could be resurrected with the "newborn." However, at this moment you could not handle that. In any case, a certain amount of information is "transmitted," from your soul to your child in the moment of conception. In that sense, your spiritual continuity is assured. It is your duty to polish that inheritance during the process of upbringing. But you have to use your own divine spark "relatively" efficiently, before you can shape another one.

As to the future of your "immortal soul" (your expression), isn't absorption in the universal-life-force an absorption in me? A unification with me? What else do you want? To dethrone me? Tough luck!

You amaze me. You admit your relativity (reluctantly I suppose) and I appreciate that. But then you require me to be almost perfect to maintain continuity in the cultivation of our divine sparks. My heart can take that because it flatters me, but my head cannot digest it because my brain has to protest against compulsion.

Where the devil is the way out?

III
The Nature of It All

Heart and head. Presumably my heart is my soul, the proprietor of that divine spark which you have endowed me with, and my head is, or should be, the logical brain, which I inherited from the apple, alias your original mistake, pardon me, your original plan, to give me a propensity for knowledge. The problem is that you have mixed them all up so badly that it is impossible to avoid an overlay, and consequent inner conflict.

You are blaming me again, while, if you wanted to be factual, you should know that in the collective philosophy of your species, both emotion and intellect have a place, albeit imperfect, yet significant even in practice. However, because of your single-minded obstinacy, which is not a divine attribute at all, you lose sight of your own results.

Maybe. But how is it possible that I have both divine and non-divine attributes? Is my psyche schizophrenic from the start? Let us say it is. Then all the prophets and preachers are liars, or brainwashed, or psychopaths. They still try to tell me that I must be a lamb, because you are omnipotent, omniscient and benevolent, and therefore you must be worshiped, or, in your "benevolence," you might bring down on me the "Wrath of God."

But your own manifestations are equally (if not more) schizophrenic than mine, and they cannot be explained by divine logic. I am told that you love me, yet you tolerate war, pestilence, poverty, murder, cruelty, and so on, probably in the name of the "great experiment." The degree of your illogical and indifferent inaction in the name of experimentation is staggering.

If you were omnipotent, then there should be no evil, because in your benevolence you would have eradicated it. But there is no evidence that you are either benevolent or omnipotent or omniscient. As a consequence, there could be room for similar powers (energy concentration with intelligence) to emerge, parallel with you, and popularly called devils. It would be easy to say that all the misery of the world is caused by devils, who also must have a boss, whom we call Satan; therefore you are not to blame.

According to Chinese cosmogony this big boss might be feminine. At the creational stages of the universe, the positive forces (yang), representing masculine "goodness" (sen), have separated from the negative forces (yin), which represented feminine "evilness" (kui), thereby determining the polarity of the Cosmos, including the heavens. With this intriguing idea they opened up a Pandora's Box of goodies, which now I am going to exploit. Satirically, of course.

By all appearances some kind of satanic forces do seem to exist, just like you seem to exist. Now: is Satan your invention, and part of the "great experiment," which got out of hand? Or is she as primeval and inexplicable as you? The "yin" of the universe? The "she-devil"! If it were a male, you could fight with it, reason with it, or compromise with it, sometimes. But with a she, you have to either hate her, or love her. When you hate her, your angels sing; when you love her, her devils cavort in a huge bacchanalia. And the earth trembles. How is this for a feminist target?

Am I right that, as you consider yourself a positive force, the "yang" of the universe, the devil must be the negative, the "yin"? (In Freudian parlance the male sexual organs must be positive, and the female negative.) And as positive and negative electrical charges attract and repulse each other, you engage in an eternal tug of war, ending up in cataclysmic orgasms, of which we are the sufferers. It is lucky that occasionally you can vent your unlimited ha-

14

tred on the devil, and satisfy your unlimited passion in her as well. (Emotions?) This way you can remain the god we cannot know, and she can remain the devil we cannot love. Perhaps it is this duality which makes up the universe! Others were speculating about that. Or perhaps, I am creating a cosmogony to suit pre-conceived images.

But what images? Certainly not Michelangelo's grandfatherly figure in the Sistine Chapel; certainly not any trinity (though functional differentiation could be one way to approach the "complexity," which I am searching for); certainly not the eternal Buddha with his purposeless Nirvana; certainly not a vengeful Yahve with his fabricated elitist legacy, certainly not Zarathustra with his homa-induced orgies; certainly not Jesus who had himself killed for Adam's apple; and certainly not Mohammed with Islam's bigoted fundamentalism. Apart from Hinduism's tolerance, and Chinese universalism's spiritual approach, there is no "form" which could be remotely acceptable as a god-concept to an agnostic. We need something, someone, whom we can personally talk to. Someone who, if not tangible, is at least comprehensible.

Then what? What is the nature of the universe? Where should we, mankind, and I, "experiment no. X," start to fathom it? What concepts / symbols should we select (very carefully), which do not lead us into a new impasse?

The thoughts you have expressed long bothered the great mystics of your species, except that in their struggle, they were more polite in contemplating the apparent conflicts of my manifestations. The mere fact that you think that we are having this conversation, and in the English idiom, which is not even your mother-tongue, presupposes that I have isolated out of my universal-life-force-self, in other words, out of the totality of my divinity an infinitesimal unit, to deal exclusively, with an even more infinitesimal unit: you, just because you have decided that it should be so.

If I were to feel emotions, I would even smile at your pretty heady presupposition. As it is, you have something there, though naturally oversimplified. Now, as you have stipulated that I am, and that there is something shared between you and me, which we agreed to call your divine spark, this common ground may be the best point of departure for you and your kind. Do not expect an early answer though. Think, like the pebble in the pond: think in terms of ever expanding, concentric circles, which represented beauty to you, till they hit shore and were destroyed. Find the wave which did not hit shore!

You vindicate me to a certain extent again, yet you are still a puzzle to me. You send me on a wild goose chase, with very little hard data. So be it. The question is how to proceed? With another question, of course, by asking myself (ignoring simpler questions, like: what the heck am I doing here?): is there an all-permeating substance in the universe, which is both harnessable, and at the same time utterly elusive?

Science would tell me that certain sub-atomic particles are so pervasive that they are practically omnipresent. Thus there is no such a thing as an "empty" space. We understand them in some of their functions, but not in their essence. To the extent that they are understood, they can probably be harnessed. Beyond that point, there are a myriad of questions. Psychics and mystics would tell me of astral bodies, life after death, telepathy, metaphysical communication, extrasensory perception, and a host of other abstract concepts, including hypnosis (which so far is the only non-physical bodily projection with scientific invocability and supportability, meaning that it can be directly induced and observed in its effects, though the process itself cannot be recorded yet). Hypnosis is also the oldest metaphysical property of the human complex, exploited by man. While the brainwaves, which accompany the hypnotic process, can be measured and exhibited in graphical forms, their interactive meaning, and the method of transmission and reception, remains an inner property of the participants. One could say though that the essence of the process is a huge loss of the critical faculty of the hypnotized. This indicates a one-sided control by the hypnotizer, over the mental state of the other, by brainwave emission to the subconscious of the hypnotized, which, then, overrides the control of his consciousness. The communication is not one-directional. While the actual instruction, to carry out a task, is almost exclusively by voice, or other sensory command, the recipient can verbalize the answers or act out the suggestions.

The nature of the trance is not fully understood. In a simple "transmittal—reception" hypnotic state, probably, only inter-participatory communication takes place between two or more "animate essences," while in mass hypnosis, a manipulated hallucinatory process dominates the subjects, governed by charismatic shamans like Moses, Buddha, Jesus, or Mohammed, etc.

In seances, where a "medium" is involved, a dreamlike state might exist, where it is rather the subconscious that is fathomed, than "messages" received from a so-called spirit world. Watch out though, for that elusive divine spark!

Religious believers would tell me that the existence of god needs no proof, because it is obviously stated in the dogmas, confirmed by the various synods. But who invented dogmas and who formalized them? Who said that they are divine revelations?

Naturally, some unscrupulous, hypocritical and power-hungry, but very brilliant humans, who wrapped their unctuousness in the benevolence of god, and protected their backsides by preaching the fear of god. Thus did take place such famous statements like those of the Council of Nicaea, which then was spread like the absolute truth. Questioning this "truth" was heresy, punishable by excommunication, or sometimes by execution.

For the unbiased observer these dogmas appeared to be unscientific, anthropomorphic, and self-serving and only believable to the uncritical mind. Nevertheless they helped the Roman Church to become a powerhouse. This condition prevailed as long as the pyramid could generate fear, and as long as increased power has brought with it increased corruption. By the onset of the Renaissance the clergy was so rotten that reaction was inevitable. Great minds questioned, attacked and rejected most of the dogmas, and made sure that they could be dumped on the garbage heap of history, which has been building, especially since the age of enlightenment, and which consisted of discarded "knowledge" and "beliefs" that accumulated throughout history.

Not that observational aphorisms cannot contain valid conclusions, but when they are replaced with intentional fabrications, and enter the area of the parapsychology, they are at best guessing and at worst lying. If, then, on top of it, they force their dictum on people they can dupe or blackmail, then they become dictatorial and forbid the human mind the practice of its most treasured property: thinking.

We are left with science and mysticism. Science acknowledges that it is approaching a point in its investigations, which, to coin a phrase, I would call "physical micro infinity." Psychics, philosophers and mystics acknowledge that they are struggling with semantics regarding the nature of the intellect, and the noetic concept of how knowledge is acquired, and where it originates from, in their effort to arrive at a definition of an intelligent, ultimate, psychic, base-energy unit, which I would call "spiritual micro infinity." I have to explain these two concepts. Generally, infinity is interpreted as something having no limit, i.e. always exceeding the value of another quantity. Micro infinity is on the other end of the scale. It represents a quantity which is infinitesimal, i.e., so small that it is almost incalculable, but always smaller than another quantity.

The smallest units science today calculates with are in the 10 mm/1,000,000/1,000,000 range. Micro infinities are considered to be beyond that, in a realm yet to be fathomed. Somewhere these two infinities must merge, and perhaps that merging point is where the true concept of godhood is hidden, and where god actually operates. And where am I in all this?

Actually on the right path. Continue searching!
What a compliment! Though, you did not remark on my "aside" on hypnotism. Can I spoil it all and finish this chapter with a statement that all prophetic actions were based on individual, and/or mass hypnosis (one divine spark against the other), creating psychological dependency between prophets and pupils? Is it possible that all our self-appointed divine messengers were really frustrated people, so disgusted with the type of nauseating, self-serving humanity around them, which they found in their lifetime, that their ministries were nothing but pent-up revenge-mechanisms released to whip the unwashed masses into a corral of religious servitude, in the name of a superior being who is to be feared, while deluding themselves with ideas of messianic missions.

Please do not answer my lord. Let me try to approach history's great shamans my own way, as I do not think that they served you well. They were acting. And, indeed, their genius as actors is undeniable. Even if sometimes they believed their own lies.

IV

Prophets and Pyramids

The son of god is the son of man. Exceptional human beings have been known to history and can but put into two main categories: (i) men who founded empires and (ii) men who founded religions.

Both discovered pretty soon that the most stable two-dimensional shape is the triangle, and the most stable solid form is the tetrahedron, the pyramid. They successfully applied these discoveries to the non-physical world as well, by creating cascading, in-line organizations, with themselves on top. This way they only had to deal with a few levels of hierarchy below them, people they knew by name. These became the immediate disciples, who rather quickly learnt the name of the game: power. The lower echelons took care of themselves by becoming adoring and zealous subordinates.

Every organization, however, must have a cohesive force to keep it together and make it work. Ideally, this force would be love in a broader sense. We know what has happened to love: individually it may still exist, but collectively it is a rarity. Therefore it cannot run either a hospital or any army, or a church. Something else is needed, or the pyramid will start to unravel, and will not grow. And growth is the essence, the destiny and the tragedy of the human race. We are willing to climb under the peak, shoulder those above us, and believe that we are doing something important. That's because we anticipate that others will force their way below us, and nurture us in the process. And so it goes, till the whole thing is a phalanstery of mindless, or at least mesmerized, masses. But something is still holding it together.

Is it idealism? Very rarely at the footsoldier's level, in an intellectual vacuum. Also idealism dies on an empty stomach and degenerates into anarchy.

What is left then? Of course fear. Fear of pain, fear of ridicule, fear of disappointment, fear of punishment, the "angoisse intellectuelle" and fear of death. The top of the pyramid, as the embodiment of the paramount portion of the conglomerate, must be feared, and if on the top of the top there is another mystical, potentially powerful something (someone), then that entity must be really feared.

And exactly that is what we are told. To repeat it: we have to fear god! Assuming of course for the sake of this scenario that there is a god.

How did this happen? Simply. The top of the pyramid has assumed the powers of the top-of-the-top, god, without really asking him whether it can do so, yet talking as if it had been commissioned to act authoritatively. Thus the great deception began.

The unquestioned and ingrained obedience, which developed from fear has kept things going, justified by the commandment of a superior being. Or so the story went and resulted in the rule of the pyramid of fear.

The subsequent, self-righteous, unctuous, and often threatening pronouncements which, in the name of god, came from the top, with reference to the prophets, held sway for a long time. But gradually some of the footsoldiers started to rebel, and shook the self-confidence of mid-management as well, thus giving room to dissatisfaction and questioning the infallibility of the tetrahedron, while the "porphyrogenety" of the churches have engaged in polemics, like how many angels can stand on the point of a needle! However, the pyramid was too strong, dismantling had to wait.

Riding on fear was no accident, because it is a frame of mind which is familiar to most of us, both through personal observation, or personal experience. But what is fear? Isn't it an irrational psychological phenomenon, which interferes with our rational thinking, and can paralyze our capability to act, if not dealt with? Or is it an escape mechanism which shifts one's inability to make decisions (like: to slice or not to slice the gordian knot) onto something outside the logical sphere of our psyche—which, nevertheless, is uncontrollably part of it—onto a "person" who we think can protect us, onto god?

When we feel threatened we often develop fear, as an acknowledgment of our weakness. In such moments god becomes terribly "existent," and governs the mind as its only solace. My god! If there is a god, help me! With this plea the bankruptcy of the intellect is completed. The individual's critical ego has been overridden by his latent superstition. What is the next step then? How can we got out of this psychological impasse? Two ways: one is by dying, if the threat was real, and no divine, or other assistance came, and the other one is by taking either instinctive or conscious evasive actions till our fear subsided, and we regain our critical faculties which enable us to analyze our situation in a reality framework. The question however remains: how did fear generate such a deep metaphysical shock in us? Because as soon as in an "angoisse intellectuelle," almost a revelation, god is evoked, i.e. as soon as an irrational statement is made on the existence of a helpful or otherwise superior being, we have to define what we mean by "existence," and what we mean by a "superior being."

By observation and introspection one must admit that perception of the world around us is possible, and that this possibility opens up the human mind to all kinds of cognitive-intellectual activities, such as understanding, thinking, learning, remembering, arguing, symbol creating and symbol manipulating; and all kinds of emotional reactions like feeling, compassion, anger, surprise, etc. The intellectual part of the process can be referred to as "noetic," which means the regression of our thoughts to their primordial base, and their examination at the level where knowledge is obtained, and ideas are born. This, still conscious, cognitive process requires extraordinary concentration, to enable one to listen to one's inner self, by letting go all scruples, hang-ups, prejudices, and preconditioned ideas. The emotional part of the process can be referred to as "orectic" which means pertaining to those functions of the mind which are not immediately controlled by our critical faculties, or analytical thinking, and are intuitive/reflective in the sense that they represent the manifestations of some imprints of our mind, which were created to react, and which were inherited from or ancestral behavior pool and experience store.

We perceive the world, we perceive existence in its many forms, and we perceive ourselves too, freely entering into polemics about it all. But a world could also exist without us, i.e., without anyone perceiving it, even though it would be a pretty futile experiment. Man, or something similar, is needed to search the universe in a meaningful manner, define its nature, and define his own role in it. And lastly, as a result of this search, he may have to postulate that a creator must be lurking somewhere in the background, because, as yet, we cannot reproduce, or at least explain, our inherent "perfection."

Interestingly, we may have arrived at our original axiom, regarding the existence of god, "a god," via this pseudo-cognitive dissertation about fear. It appears that it is through fear that we experience that emotional anguish, which reaches down to our subconscious and evokes the age-old longing for some support of the unknown, who/which is, if not omni, but potent enough to rescue us, even if the whole thing is nothing but deep-rooted superstition. Fear is an animal trait, and we have inherited it from our evolutionary ancestors, who shuddered and cowered when lightning struck too close. Fear is also tied to the preservation of the self and the species, and was used as a disciplinary measure by all messiahs, including Jesus. Thus, this extraordinary cement, fear, has whipped us into obedience, subordinated faith to religion, any religion, and ensured that pyramid-building can begin and succeed.

Of course, this could only happen if some men were more equal than others, and used their superiority to their own end. It is the cruelty, and also the genius of evolution that all men were not born equal. In the system which developed from this premise, there was no need to think or understand, only to humble oneself, believe, toe the line, and pray. And of course fear.

This went on for a long time and for most people. But, eventually, the divine spark, which is unquestionably part of us (another existential observation) had started to come to the surface, and assert itself in a rebellious way, especially as the top of the pyramid has become rotten, and the critical faculty of many minds has realized that there is something wrong in Rome. At this time man has started to question himself about existence as such, and superiority as a concept, because he was unhappy with his "inferiority." Descartes drafted it well. "Dubito ergo cogito, cogito ergo sum." If this is so, i.e., "I exist," then, if I convinced myself of this existence by the complex process of "doubt," and start thinking further, I can understand and explain other existences as well. Therefore, if "existence" is the observable (tangible or intangible) materialization or manifestation of recombinant basic, building blocks of the universe, the observer being both the effector and the effectee, then the mutual perception and noetization of heterogeneous existential phenomena should lead us to the understanding of what we call life, in all its appearances and aspects. Thus the flower which opens to the sunlight; the mosquito that stings your arm; the antelope which is chased by the lion are all existence-perception manifestations of life events, unreported but actual. It is only man who can conceptualize and subsequently formalize and record the interaction between those events, and comment on their cause-and-effect relationship. In addition, he can project his observations in any direction he likes. As regards "superiority," let us say that man has consciously succeeded in perceiving himself, and, at least partially, in explaining himself. In this process, however, he became dissatisfied with some of his own arguments and postulated that he is not alone in the universe. He could not prove it but by a series of natural coincidences, like volcanic eruptions, meteorites from the sky, earthquakes, etc., he concluded that something must be controlling these frightening occurrences. He started to speculate, about what he could not explain, started to spin stories, and to support his stories, he collected some unusual-looking objects, endowed them with magical powers, and created fetishes. From this "achievement," it was only a refinement to appoint shamans, and invent superior beings, like gods. By elevating something/someone above himself, man has conceptualized superiority. The prophets were masters of this game.

Actually, in not a few instances, man has declared himself "god," and pre-empted the privilege of the existing, polytheistic pantheons, by stealing godhood from previous "legitimate" owners of the title. However, when the currently ultimate form of godhood, a monotheistic god, became widely accepted, he had to lower his sight and satisfy himself with the role of "supreme" representative of the almighty. But by that time, his subconscious thirst for solving a mystery, has prompted him to "up-the-ante" and challenge god on the basis of his own divine spark; challenge the "system" on the basis of his ability to use logic, and on the basis of an uneasy inner feeling that he was being fooled. The pyramid has started to shed its cladding, and the prophets of ancient times are only remembered by the decaying structures they created many, many centuries ago.

V

Origin, Identity, Image

To challenge god, man had to define god. After innumerable trials and errors, man concluded that god is a spiritual being, who must be superior to him, must be all pervasive, must, or should be benevolent, omnipotent and omniscient. And if all this is true, god must be revered, respected and worshiped. With these definitions, or characterizations if you like, man has laid the cornerstone of his own psychological and moral enslavement to dogmatic thinking. Man has never asked god if he is searching for his, god's, own identity, image, or origin. Man has never found out if god has put him in his laboratory to determine what thought, and the ability to use excessive emotion and limited logic together, will develop into. Man has never asked god for an explanation of the reason for his existence, as somehow, god and existence were tied together in the fable of creation.

Most likely, man was put here to think for god and struggle with the existential imperative of the age-old, man-god relationship, trying to bridge the intellectual abyss which separates us, and trying to formulate a believable image for him. While god said that he has no image, we are still looking for one, because a being without an image is a contradiction in non-spiritual terms. In our search we might eventually be able to sufficiently circumscribe him, to construct a projection of him. This will be a rather high achievement on man's part, especially if it could be done in a way which is divorced from "religious"-type thinking. How to achieve godhead then? Or half-godhead? Or shall I just continue searching? I am exhausted. Now let me hear you my lord!

Here and there you have made logical errors, but in general your effort is commendable. However, before, I remark on your ramblings, let me make one thing clear: based on our earlier exchanges, we touched on the possibility that I, as your god, can take any form or shape I like, and communicate with you accordingly. I can separate a specific unit out of my infinity, and probably that's what I am doing now, not to overwhelm you. I could say that you are talking to one of my "angelic" manifestations, but you don't believe in angels, and you are right. I could say that the "holy ghost" has descended upon you, but I would get a sarcastic remark from you. So, let us just say that you are talking to your own divine spark, as in that we have something in common. We can dismiss angels who sing my glory in heaven, as there is no heaven, period. Especially not of your description. I would be a masochist to accept that! Heaven and hell is your story, and you experience them in your present life, on this speck of dirt which you call earth. But as your earth is still huge in comparison with the infinitely small building blocks of the universe, you have plenty of room to fight your battles, though you may have noticed that your world has shrunk. Even if you colonized the planets in your galaxy, you would be still so insignificant in the billions of galaxies, that you should stop and think.

(By the way, you better start colonizing other, habitable planets, soon.) In your insignificance, however, you have one redeeming feature, which needs constant emphasis: your divine spark, which is the essence of your life and your intelligence. Your future will depend on how well you will be able to enhance and increase that spark in yourself. The supply is infinite. You wanted to become god! Did you not? Go to it! Don't get carried away though! The vastness around you should render you modest, rather than boastful of your achievements.

Nevertheless, as you have developed some entertainable

ideas in your search, I have decided to expand on my statement regarding you talking to your own divine spark. If that spark is part of infinity, then it can access it too. Thus the conversation you are "experiencing" is not the result of me isolating and assigning a spiritual unit of myself to enter into an argument with you. Rather it is an extension of your spirituality through the courage of your own mental excursion into the unknown, to understand better my universe, even if the whole process takes place in your head. This type of mental exercise you can handle, because it is essentially part of your intellectual make-up.

Talking of that part of the universe, which you said I have created (am I telling you something here?), our comparison of it to a laboratory will suffice for now, and we may return to it. Your question regarding my identity, image and origin however should be examined in the light of that eternal paradox: did mind create matter, or did recombinant matter "manufacture" mind? Or are both only different manifestations of what you have aptly called the basic building blocks of the universe? Your "infinities"?

Let us start with my origin, the most puzzling question. Did I have this all-pervasive presence rooted in eternity, so long ago that not even I can remember it? Or was my origin suppressed in that concentrated, mindless energy ball, which I had to blow up to start the universe? And was there another creator before me, who collapsed everything into that cosmic black hole, which your scientists tell you was the origin of the world, in order that it can explode, or I can explode it? Was it a sort of a punishment which I had to suffer because of some "primeval" wrongdoing? Or did I collapse the universe that existed before this universe into that "recent" black hole, imprisoning myself in it as well, because I was dissatisfied with the old one? These questions can be asked infinitely, and, truthfully, I do not know the answer. This many surprise you. Riddles of this magnitude have not been encountered in your history, and now you have to try to digest them.

Perhaps you can help your god to solve this "cross-world-

puzzle," if it is solvable at all. One thing however is to your advantage: when I endowed you with that infinitesimal tool, the divine spark, and diversified you to use it on my behalf, I was not fully cognizant of the possibility, that you might develop excessive emotions, as a primary determinant factor of your psyche, instead of a secondary one.

You properly observed that divine logic has no compassion, does not feel pain, and is not moved by sentiment. But, when in your evolutionary process you started to develop concepts and feelings, like: love, hate, sorrow, anger, sympathy, etc., you have derailed and misused your divine spark, and entered on a road of conflict with me, or actually your own image of me. Do you see a paradox here?

This conflict has never been resolved, and the substitute "solutions," the so-called religions of the world, which you invented, have never brought you that inner contentedness or happiness which you strive for. It has only brought you division and strife and a series of metaphysical impasses. You said that you were told that I am merciful, but that is a fabrication. You said your god loves you, but that concept is not part of godhood. As your god, I am running a universe, not a kindergarten. However, as I am a logical being, I must expose also non-godly ideas to logical analysis. Therefore, I must ask myself (perhaps as a result of this imaginary conversation with you . . .), why I don't place more emphasis on emotions? Is it possible that when I gave away a spark of myself, I created a situation not unlike to that, which occurred when I gave the universe its basic rules: I have fortuitously built into the system the possibility of accidents, as I burst into a "space" which existed before me, or at least with me. Similarly, when I created you through evolution, and equipped you with a part of me, I brought about a being, who may develop his own concepts and even challenge me. Perhaps, and only perhaps, I might be able to learn something from you, and adjust the world, your world, to reduce ingrained conflicts in your species. It is a huge task, because, as you remarked, I cannot change fully developed individuals with ease, I have to go back to the micro-infinity level (your expression), and therefore work through a number of generations.

In summary, my primordial origin is just as much a mystery to me as to you, except for the probability that I have better theories about it than you. You are getting impatient! Just wait a little! I am going to return to this subject occasionally, but first I would like to tell you a possible impossibility. Being confined in the cosmic black hole, and then released (so to speak) in the "Big Bang" could have either erased or absorbed some memory traces of my past and, therefore, at least some of my "relative" (your expression again) being is a "Tabula Rasa." Therein lies the contradictory nature of my origin, and the vulnerability of my complex, which, no doubt, you will point out.

My identity was the next question you wanted an answer for. If by identity you mean "distinctive character," then you have to decide if distinction is more important to you than character, or if you would like to fuse the two. In any case you have to refer back to earlier chapters of our discussion, when you tried to explain the concept of god, and tried to understand existence. Tough job, because I am neither directly observable in my manifestations, nor have I materialized for you, to behold my apparition.

While, to see me is your species' most ardent wish, you are not going to have that pleasure: remember, I have no image! Thus, my character is, at least for now, beyond human explanation, and therefore it is unique and distinct, and certainly not anthropomorphic. This, however, should not stop you from theorizing about me.

If I wanted to describe myself to you, I would say that I am a combination of the universal-life-force which permeates all, and that supreme, creative spirituality, which overrides the world's "free-radical" energy, and controls what you can only conceptualize as the divine process. Here, life-force is to be interpreted as the physical "state," where morphic resonance keeps everything moving—(your panta rei)—in an ever-expanding continuum; and spirituality is to be interpreted as the intelligent macro-nucleus of my being. Life-force can also be interpreted as a multitude of energized universal building blocks, absorbed in my spirituality, and doing the bidding of my divine decisions. Of course my divinity I have inherited from my own creator, even if I was that creator. This is another paradox for you: how could I have created myself?

Quite easily, because I am distinct from all concepts that you can dream up, and I can renew myself cataclysmically or otherwise, or, like a phoenix, emerge from the fire of transformation which tried to subdue or consume my earlier life. Thus it is the creator, who was the creator of the creator. It does not make human sense; does it? But it should not worry you at this moment: if you achieve a "relative" theory which would help replacing religious morality with the morality which is dictated by your divine spark, you would have done your job.

The last aspect of my being which you were musing about is my image. This is an elusive one, as it does not really exist. When you gave me an image in terms of a superior entity and juxtaposed this entity with another entity, the "devil," you oversimplified the role of positive and negative forces in the universe. You even went so far as to call them good and bad. You did not realize that I had no choice over their existence, as they form the very, inner substance of me on the one hand, and represent the tools of my executive will on the other. By now you must sense that nothing can be absolute (one of your correct observations) except nothingness itself, and nothingness is indefinable, once we accept that reality exists. In an absence of reality communication cannot take place. You could also say that nothingness is the absence of reality. In this case you have almost defined it, but you cannot do much with it, because it is not in that milieu that you want to build your concept of the universe, and it is meaningless for me too, because I consist of "something," even if I don't have an image.

Your efforts to give me one are therefore futile. This means that you should not even try to state that I am "omni" this, or "omni" that. You are much better off if you question me, or even attack me, because I can understand your desire for knowledge. That is why I am talking to you, instead of trying to order you to worship me.

I appreciate your audacity much more than the unctuousness of your reprehensible, religious representatives, whom I do not find particularly intelligent. I equally despise the opportunism of proselytes, and the self-serving, self-glorifying boastfulness of your church potentates.

I respect the divine spark in you, because it is part of the universal-life-force, it is part of me, and in that sense it is my equal at your level of consciousness. That I could not create you to be perfect, or rather, that I had to create you imperfect, because of the scale of your existence, is one of the reasons why you took off in your development in an ungodly direction, giving a new twist to my experimentation with you.

Thanks a lot! Of course, I am to blame! So be it! Nevertheless, you have given me some further food for thought. Enough to dive into a little pseudo-historic "reasoning," to try to put things in perspective.

But isn't it the description of a "perspective" explanation of the universe or the relative importance of the facts about it, what I have been trying to arrive at all along? How much more "perspective" can a man be than to acknowledge the existence of god, and at the same time to attempt to establish kinship with him?

Did I not already break out of the clutches of anthropomorphic thinking when I called god indefinable, the universe a puzzle, mankind an experiment, religion a power play, the churches irrelevant and all churchmen charlatans?

I think I did. But at the same time I have created a vacuum into which no one dares to jump. I will also only tip-toe into it.

Let us see why the creation of a religionless but not godless vacuum was necessary. (Here is another paradox for you: if there is a god, then god fills all, and there is no vacuum. But there is still a vacuum in human terms, because we need a definable and positive philosophy of life.) Let us start with a little history, and let us see what it can teach us.

VI

T'ai Ki: The Ancient Beginning

Initially, man, and almost without exception the male of the species, tried intuitively, to explain things which he did not understand, and formulated ideas and beliefs which appeared to be supported by random coincidences. In a creekbed the sun shone on a piece of quartz which reflected its rays in a rainbow pattern. He took the stone home. This act of his was followed by a few lucky events in hunting, and the stone became a fetish. The other hunters noticed this and brought home stones of their own. Our first fetish finder could not tolerate that and, as he was the strongest, he subdued the others, confiscated their stones, and declared himself the true keeper of "the" stone, a shaman.

A little later Moses came down the mountain with two pieces of stones and bamboozled the Israelites with the message of god. As he was an Egyptian, perhaps the son of a beautiful Jewish concubine and a Pharaoh or of an Egyptian princess and a handsome Jewish scribe (you can take your pick), he was exposed to the work of the masterful stonemasons who carved and sculpted Egypt's awe-inspiring monuments. Also, as children, young Egyptians were playing with stones, hammers and chisels, and the more talented ones were selected for training. Carving as an art form was extremely important to the ruling classes of Egypt, and therefore it is imaginable that Moses got some training too, and could have carved the basic behavioral norms of his Jewish brethren into his tablets, for history.

Indeed he must have been a great shaman. But already before him, thinkers like Japhet, Sem, Ham, and Abraham had experimented with morality of some sort, and the Hindus (Brahma has intellectualized shamanism), the Chinese, and the Egyptians reached a fairly high level of religio-philosophic sophistication, preparing the ground for the emergence of Jesus, and the meteoric rise of Mohammed, the last of the great religion-makers.

We should step back, however, and try to establish a relative chronology of prophetic activities. In this context let me briefly describe the characteristics of a human being whom we could accept as a major prophet. (Minor prophets, though numerous, need not concern us here, because they did not inspire world religions.)

Essentially, prophets are visionaries, who developed a messianic fervor, convincing themselves that they have been divinely selected to provide for the so-called spiritual needs of their people. They successfully achieved this aim, using their hypnotic, charismatic personality, influencing some impressionable and some unscrupulous people, to whom they preached their gospels, to follow them unconditionally. (This shows what your divine spark can do.)

The formalization of the teachings of these extraordinary men usually only happened after their death, when even more unscrupulous people, riding on a band-wagon, organized their fellow-travellers into self-serving, tightly knit, but initially neighborly units, which later divested themselves of all their neighborly characteristics, and became dogmatic religions, driving their adherents into intellectual and moral slavery. Thus was the "globalization" of man's spiritual craving achieved. Religions have become the trade unions of faith. Why was this process, which repeated itself in many cultures, necessary? Why was it necessary to create irrational and essentially fear-governed bodies to take over man's exclusive right to communicate with his god? How could superstition-based dogmas suppress the divine spark in so many of our forebears and contemporaries? And for so long? How could charismatic charlatans stunt the development of human thought, and consequently ensure that base human characteristics remain virtually unchanged through the millennia? What core of our psyche did these exceptional prophets touch to make religions and their sister-philosophies: extreme ideologies, influence us in such a way that under their banner we have become the greatest mass murderers of history, and at the same time inspire self-sacrifice to such a degree that believers in them would gladly die in the process? Are these the inscrutable ways of the creator, our lord and father? If so, then this would make him a rather unpleasant father.

Or did the self-appointed representatives of the creator-image, the Brahmas, Moseses, Buddhas, Zarathustras, Jesuses and Mohammeds, etc., misuse their divine spark, their god-given genius, by fooling humanity into believing in anthropomorphic heavenly hierarchies, which without the element of fear would collapse? Or are they really messengers of god? How did we get into this mess of religious proliferation, which does not seem to lead us anywhere?

What beginning did we have to have and when, to eventually progress, almost shoulder-to-shoulder, toward diverse, but essentially parallel, theocentric societies? What triggered the emergence of our intelligence?

As an illustration let us look at the Fourth Millennium B.C., the early period of recorded history (creationists beware and remember centuries in evolution mean very little!):

4000 B.C. (give or take a few centuries):

EGYPT:	The early dynasty of the pharaohs was already well-established.
MESOPOTAMIA:	Cuneiform writing was already in use.
CRETE:	The Minotaur was already feeding on beautiful girls.
INDIA:	The Dravidians and Arians were already descending into the Indus Valley, Mohenjo Daro and Harappa were flourishing. The seeds of Hinduism were sewn.
CHINA:	Fu Hi the first "Jade Emperor" was already speculating about the Yang and the Yin of the Universe.
EUROPE:	The construction of Stonehenge has already started.
AMERICA:	The cultivation of maize has already been in progress.

It is possible that, when God programmed the sequence of life on earth, in the ancient beginning (we don't know about the rest of the universe), he set the genetic clock of future living things in such a way that first bacteria then protozoa, fish, reptiles, mammals and primates came on stream by predetermined, timed mutations, and at last the human animal's genes were triggered (in their many forms: white, brown, and black) to step out of their pre-Cro-Magnon existence and became true homo sapiens. Some say that mutation has not been observable in recorded history. Have they talked to microbes lately? Did they not notice that microbes have the advantage over us? Someone even said that there is no proof, that the world has not been created for the sake of bugs? They represent more numerous life forms than anything else, and more durable ones too. Their generation time is minutes instead of years. They evolve rapidly and mutate easily to become antidote resistant. They keep rearranging their old genomes, to come up with new ways to overcome our defences. As regards timing, we don't have to go far. We only have to look at the process from conception to birth, to death. Everything is timed, in most cases almost perfectly. Aberrations will usually abort, or result in miscreants. (Nowadays we pamper them; the Spartans used

37

to throw them down the Taigetos.) (Natural selection?) In those of us who survived, first, growth is triggered, then teeth, then puberty, then maturity, and at last old age and death. (As an example: has anyone seen puberty setting in before a child got his or her second set of teeth?)

In geological time our life span doesn't mean even seconds. In evolutionary time a few hours. In historical time a few years. Thus it was not human existence that was created 8,000 to 6,000 or so years ago, but the time came for the intelligence-genomes of our ancestors' gene pool to be activated, enabling stone-age man to evolve into metal-age man, and into homo sapiens sapiens. This means that god was working at the micro infinity level, and that we don't have to be ashamed of our quasi animal ancestry, because, in our totality, we have been long destined to become human.

This has been said before, but it needs repeating, because only a few are listening. The next step in the evolutionary process may be, hopefully, that time may trigger genes which control violence. God's laboratory is still active, and so should be ours. We have a lot of catching up to do. The race is not won yet. Perhaps we should try to separate out these recalcitrant genes, and surprise god by substituting some of our emotional/violence genes with logical ones. Brave new world . . .

But let us get back to the era when men were already communicating in sentences as well as in words, and in some cases, developed rudimentary attempts at writing.

It was about five to seven thousand years ago that individuals started to conceptualize the world around them. At that time humanity was bereft of earlier thoughts (unless instructed by extraterrestrials), and ranged free in the newly discovered domain of abstract thinking.

In this process, in a remote corner of Asia, Hinduism was born, developing into one of the most tolerant and open-minded imagery, regarding the abstract and inexplicable parts of the universe around us, and our place in it. This relative free-love with the spiritual world did not last long, in its purest form. The brahmas were followed by the brahmins, and other "men of god," a bunch of increasingly more dogmatic practitioners of deception, starting a process, which was copied by latter-day prophets and messiahs.

The long chain of "prophetic" events, at this moment not considering geographic locations, could be best represented by a spiral, which grows with the expanding universe. To make it more interesting, I have combined it with the Chinese symbol for the "ancient beginning" the "T'ai Ki," at a stage when the positive (yang), and negative (yin) forces have already separated. In our cosmology I could compare that to the first micro-second of the "Big Bang."

The diagram below shows a clock of selected prophetic, etc., phenomena during the past 100,000 years. The sequence is historically as good as I could get it. Some of the dates are still debated by archeologists and historians. It does not matter for our purpose. In general terms the clock is right, and shows, that after Mohammed no major prophets have emerged, unless you call Lenin, Stalin and company, the prophets of extreme ideologies. These, now historical, personalities represented the deepest aberration of the human spirit, and probably the greatest degree of cruelty committed by man against man, in the name of a quasi-religious, but atheistic ideology, communism.

It appears that history's possible great dramas have all been played out. The future can only be repetitious. Unless our divine spark prevails. In the meantime, shall we see how our story looks on the T'ai Ki scale?

Time Spiral

The relation of the "Prophetic Era" to selected events and personalities of world history or the progression of mankind's philosophical speculations from fetishistic theism through materialistic A - theism to scientific - cum - spiritual metaphysical morality.

WU KI

THE ETERNAL EXISTENCE

THE PROPHETIC ERA
(2000 B.C. - 500 A.D.)

← A.D. B.C. →

JESUS

T'AI KI

SYMBOL OF THE ANCIENT BEGINNING

40

VII

The Development of the Cosmos

An Oriental View

1. The Timeless Era.

The Chinese world-view had postulated a neutral, "Ur-alt," state for the origin of the universe, in other words, a state of eternal existence, presumably in complete balance and harmony. They called this state the "Wu Ki," and represented it by a simple circle. Chinese philosophers, with their proverbial, inscrutable smile stood back from an explanation of it. Modern philosophers are still struggling with it.

2. The Creative Era.

From this "Ur-alt" state, the "Tao," the "ancient cause" also containing the "universal and unifying world law," has separated out the positive and negative primeval forces (the Big Bang) to begin their work. The white and black design, the T'ai Ki, in the above sketch represents the separated state of the once unified forces symbolizing the interdependence of the polarities, in an eternally changing, yet unified cosmos. Another symbolism is the identification of the positive forces (yang) with masculine "good-

41

ness" (sen), and the negative forces (yin) with feminine "evilness" (kui).

3. The Cooling Period.

The "conflicts" of the T'ai Ki event have been with us for 9,000,000,000 years and brought about constant expansion till our planet cooled down adequately for life to appear. After that, another long evolutionary period, about 4 billion years, had to elapse for humanoids to develop from amino acids, etc., into neolithic man. This happened about 10,000 years ago, in the Holocene epoch. The 6 days of the "creation" took about 13 billion years, and the expansion still continues.

4. The Evolutionary Era.

The earth is about 4.5 billion years old. The oldest rocks on earth are about 4 billion years old. Shortly after (in geological terms), when the first rocks had solidified, and water had formed protozoa appeared God started the creation of life. Man, in his Australopithecus form, only evolved 4.5 million years ago.

5. The Dominance of Man.

This era was supposed to have started about 130,000 years ago, indicating that the Chinese had more "courage" in speculating about a possible time for a creation, than the writers of the Old Testament.

This time period is uncannily close to modern science's contention that "Steinheim man," a "progressive" Neanderthaler, perhaps the first homo sapiens, lived about 130,000 years ago, descending from homo erectus. Cave-paintings go back 30,000 years. By this time man has evolved to his modern physique.

6. The Present.

The last 12,000 years the Chinese consider historical times, beginning with the Stone Age. Around this time village structures started to appear. By 8000 B.C., man had been working with clay, and by 6000 B.C. was producing some metals as well. After 4000 B.C., the progress of the human race has accelerated, and among others produced the Chinese sages and our prophets. And eventually us.

This brief summary of cosmic history has been included here in graphic form as well as in text, to give an overview to what follows; to show the minuscule nature of our existence, when compared to the Universe; and to admire the human mind for its ability to conceptualize it. (See Chapter VI.) The past has been condensed, the present stretched out; and the future just hinted at. Selected events of the last 100,000 years, combined with the "Wu Ki" and the "T'ai Ki," are shown. The essence of the diagram is that all major prophetic phenomena took place in "the shadowy depths of recorded history," in a relatively narrow time corridor (3,500 years between Brahma and Mohammed), where legends of the past were the rules and facts were the exceptions. Our great prophets made a mess of the facts, by substituting fables for them. Prophets have seldom produced visual art, but exhibited great genius in their attempt to write, or inspire "Vedic," etc., poetry. This "sacred knowledge," which was therefore also a secret knowledge (they knew that it was a figment of their imagination), enabled them to declare their stories divine in origin, and themselves messengers of god.

It was too long a time and too great an effort for evolution to produce a bunch of self-centered story-tellers. At least the Chinese produced Confucius! If the measure is the number of people they managed to influence, none of the philosophers/prophets of Western Eurasia had the same influence, in his time as he had. Not even Plato or Aristotle. Jesus had not been born yet when Confucius had already institutionalized morality.

The approximate time-table of the prophets is as follows: (Where uncertainties exist, I am showing extremes.)

2900–2000	B.C.	Brahma
1590–1250	B.C.	Moses
1200–550	B.C.	Zarathustra
560–480	B.C.	Buddha
550 B.C.–480	B.C.	Confucius
2 B.C.–33	A.D.	Jesus
570–632	A.D.	Mohammed

In summary, the fact that in that last 1390 years no new, major prophets have emerged (in the ancient beginning of recorded history every 500 years or so have produced one) may mean two things:

   a. either we have exhausted the supply of religious innovations; or

   b. mankind cannot be fooled any more, to the same extent as before.

(Though, the many "sects" that plague humanity today would indicate otherwise. Or, some people just want to be fooled.)

Don't you agree my lord?

Your animosity to your prophets is not logical. You are doing the same thing they have done in their time, expanding their thoughts in the direction of least resistance: upwards. Actually, when you blame the prophets, your quarrel is not really with them, but with lesser individuals who followed them in time, seized the day, and took over control, recognizing the real values in the prophets' prolific preachings and turning these values to their advantage. You mentioned pyramids and structures; those represented to you organizational attempts to make order out of chaos, assume power, and keep the machinery running. This kind of endeavor is widespread on your planet, and you can observe it from ants to plants. The fault does not lie there. The fault lies in the free-will aspect of your being. You think that just because you have a free will component in your cognitive make-up, you can give free rein to it too. Your emotions still rule your intellect, most of the time, and lead you to biased conclusions. You are suggesting I accept emotions as part of my divinity. (I trust, you know that I know about them.) I am asking you to apply more logic. Let us see if you will do better, when you examine your great adversaries. In a sense they all reached me, let us see now if they can reach you. They were giants of your species, and started out with great promises. You will say they failed. I do not think so, because the experiment is not over yet, and the ultimate synthesizer of all prophetic philosophies has not been born yet. Or has he?

Harsh words. But I have to bow to your argument for the moment, as I am just about to start analyzing their enduring essence. Let me reserve judgment to the end of my work, because I would like to base my opinions on the evidence I can obtain.

On then with our prophets.

VIII
Brahma—2900 B.C.

This prophetic name may not cover one single man. It may only have been a generic term, to personify an idea which appeared to have divine origin. But gods do not descend to earth, yet we like to conceptualize metaphysical entities, and identify them in human terms, because we think like humans, and we like human achievements. It must have been fun to create gods and to make people believe that they are real.

The deeper in time we dig into the verity of historic personalities, the more we find their existence entwined in legend, occasionally endowing them with divine, or at least spiritually conceived and materialized origin. This is the case with the Hindu trinity as well, where Brahma, Vishnu and Shiva represent personifications of three, supposed divine realities. If such personification is based on some exceptional, real people, whose life stories were gradually embellished through ancestor worship and story-spinning, then we are not faced with a dilemma. But, if these "prophets" of antiquity have undergone a subsequent deification process, then we have to drag them back to earth, and respect them not as demigods, but as human geniuses of their time, whose insight gave a segment of mankind centuries worth of inspired thoughts, in this case about Hinduism.

The thoughts which characterize Hinduism center around the tenet that it is not necessary to believe in a transcendent god; it is acceptable to be an atheist, a panentheist or a theist. It is up to the individual to choose. Salvation can be achieved, if that is one's goal, in many ways, as the "sansara," the eternal rotation, the "panta-rei" of the animate essence of the world, gives several chances to the transmigrating soul, through "recycling."

This tremendous metaphysical freedom is in sharp contrast with the rigid caste system, which is the foundation of Hindu society. This is based on the observed fact that all creatures are not equal at all. The "Dharma," or "universal law," or "spiritual imperative" which governs the constantly evolving material and intellectual complex, which we call our universe, has neither a beginning nor an end. Its effect is manifested in differentiation, and not in uniformity. This heterogeneous view of the cosmos, however, does not exclude the existence of a homogeneous "Karma" or acquired fate of an individual, which he, as an animate unit, has deserved through action. Part of this "Karma" is also born with you, and forms a person's frame of existence, from where it can only escape through reincarnation. The lack of spiritual bondage, and the tolerance implied by it, makes Hinduism one of the most attractive metaphysical philosophies of the world. It is a pity that it has been tied into knots by the brahmins, in their millennia old struggle for near hegemony over the Indian peninsula.

They perpetuated an exclusive social order for their own benefit, while pigeonholing a vast portion of the Hindu nation. They placed themselves on an exalted intellectual plane: the only ones who can interpret the Vedas; and thereby denied the freedom of choice to the rest of the population. They denied the very thing they were supposed to protect and promote. With this they have lost the admiration of the thinking/scientific world, which is in the process of probing the secrets of the universe, trying to reconcile quantum physics and the general theory of relativity with the existence of god.

Nevertheless, the pure philosophy of Hinduism still represents that intellectual platform, upon which a noetic/logical approach to understanding "godhead" could be built, if we divested it of the ritualistic nonsense, which the brahmins have invented to control their people. The interesting thing is, that while the brahmins did not build a religious hierarchy, they did build a unique social order with irreconcilable boundaries, which they managed to shape to act as a substitute for theocracy. As a consequence Hinduism became the least religious of all religions, and therefore deserves further attention, as it has developed on three principles, which appear to have stood the test of time, at least for Hindus:

1. The "Dharma," the "eternal cause," the "absolute," which governs the universe;
2. The "Karma," the "fate, deserved by action," which governs the individual; and
3. The "gods," who obey the Dharma and interact with the Karma.

To further characterize Hinduism, we could put down three points:

i) Hinduism was not founded by one man, like Christianity, or Islam, and was not the result of divine revelation in any form either. It has "evolved" through the centuries, and it was only interpreted by great minds like Brahma, Vishnu and Shiva; and by later wise men. As a consequence it is an eternal religion, a world-law, or "sanatana Dharma," which teaches the eternity of a self-perpetuating universe (with or without a creator), but under the aegis of an all-permeating, governing power. In this universe, gods, who themselves are subject to reincarnation, play only a limited intermediate part.

ii) Hinduism grants freedom to the individual to follow or shape his destiny (Karma), and does not build up strict dogmas to regulate religious belief and behavior. Hinduism has no anthropomorphic origin; it has no personalized, Moses-like shamans. Brahma has only collected the eternal sacred books, the "Vedas," and Vishnu and Shiva are only parts of a recurring phenomenon, a reincarnation of ancient sages, who periodically emerge to continue the task of spiritual teaching.

iii) Hinduism is not missionary, in the sense that it does not accept non-Hindus (with probably increasing exceptions) into its midst. Yet Hindus emphasize the superiority and eternity of the tenets of the Vedas, which the prophetic persons of the times interpret, update, and modernize to suit the circumstances and mentality of a particular age. The Hindu considers that the Vedas contain the eternally valid principles of our world, which must govern thought and action at all times. The keepers, interpreters and moderators of these principles are the brahmins.

These condensed characteristics of Hinduism imply an openness of mind concerning the existence and form of an ultimate being, or spiritual reality in a metaphysical transcendency, or in any other context. They also imply a closed mind toward humanity, despite the fact that homo sapiens are the only known reality on earth (and perhaps at all) that can perceive themselves; can express this perception; and then can postulate abstract concepts like transcendency, and can even understand them to a certain extent too. The contradictory duality of the Hindu complex: privilege and caste, is almost divine in its inequity, as it favors the 1 percent over the 99 percent.

But when Hindus talk of an "eternal cause," they touch on the field of inquiry which is the subject of these studies. Whether such an eternal cause can be isolated from the harsh reality of the caste system is yet to be seen. But in Hinduism everything appears to be possible (hence its attractiveness), as it has managed to reconcile the theist, the agnostic, the atheist, and the dialectic materialistic viewpoints, as long as the individual subscribing to these philosophies obeys the moral principles laid down by the "sanatana Dharma." Therein lies Hinduism's longevity.

In an incredibly brilliant "tour-de-force," the brahmin gave their followers almost unlimited freedom regarding their metaphysical beliefs, or the lack of such beliefs, while incarcerating them in a jail-strong social structure. This way they were able to set themselves above lower castes, and give the impression that they have nothing to do with everyday politics, as the existing order, which they have perpetrated, is of divine origin. Their job is to interpret the Vedas. They are not responsible for human misery. This way, as in every well-established hierarchy, they achieved the enslavement of the masses, for the benefit of the few.

From the aforegoing it could be concluded that the social achievements of Hinduism are not terribly social at all, neither are they prone to improve the position and the mentality of the grassroots. The only bright light in the inherited regimentation of the non-spiritual life of India lies in the emphasis that the caste system, in the ultimate analysis is of limited nature, and is subject to the "sansara," the eternal rotation of the universe, and can be escaped by a complete rejection of the mundane. Such asceticism will elevate the practitioner over all castes, and their laws and restrictions.

What, then, are the spiritual achievements of Hinduism?

Perhaps, some of the answers could be drafted as follows:

1. While branded as a religion, in actual fact, it has avoided becoming a religion, because it has no compulsory dogmas.
2. It has managed to maintain a philosophy, which does not condemn the individual to intellectual slavery.
3. It has stipulated that the world could exist without a god, yet hints at the potential existence of a pantheon of superior intelligences, over whom only the universal spirit rules, in an incomprehensible manner.
4. It acknowledges its prophets, like Brahma, Vishnu, Shiva, etc., on a human scale, but does not deny the believers their right to worship them as demigods, or even gods.
5. It acknowledges that the sacred books need interpreta-

tions, and that these interpretations must be constantly upgraded and updated, i.e. they must be dynamic and not static.

6. To attain this aim, the emergence of latter-day prophets is required in every age, they will maintain Hinduism's flexibility, and ensure that the caste system will not lose its inflexibility. (In this they have pre-dated Orwell.)

This summary of Hinduism's achievements was written in the framework of the original presupposition of the first book of this trilogy, namely that there is a god. Therefore we should ask him, how he would regard this most ancient world-view? Of course, we should not forget that small things, like Brahmanism/Hinduism may not be substantial enough subjects for him to deserve a comment. But I have to ask: how now my lord?

Your sarcasm aside, the earth, your world, is still one of my experiments. You asked if there are other planets with intelligent life on them? Possibly. But, as I said you have to find that out for yourself. In the meantime, none of your so-called religions, or ideologies, or cosmologies have dealt with the question: What would happen if human life did not exist? Or became extinct? And only animal, plant, and bacterial life remained on earth? Who would conceptualize gods, and who would worship them? The answer is that this world of yours and mine would be a rather futile experiment without someone able to perceive it, in its total beauty and complexity, and even to argue with me. I trust that you don't consider me stupid enough to go through another creative-evolutionary journey of a few million years, just to annihilate you, because of the convoluted development of your psyche. No! I will allow my experiments to run their courses because, as in all processes, there is a tendency for balance built into the universe that, sometimes with self-generated cataclysmic events, and sometimes with natural inertia will eradicate exces-

51

sive aberrations, the limit of which your own divine spark will determine.

As diversification was one of the criteria which I selected for my earthly experiments, the philosophy which you called Hinduism got off to a relatively good start. Describing my sublime reality, which permeates the world, as "the eternal cause" is an apt symbolism of the divine essence, even, if in the next sentence they deny, or at least question, the existence of a creative and managing entity. They love paradox, but they keep an open mind. In your terms, they respect the value in the saying that thought must not be shackled. Thus, it is the intellectual level of Hinduism which is most inspired, as it permits the development and expression of wide-ranging ideas. No matter how audacious or outrageous these ideas are, they must be entertained, until logical, divine arguments refute them. As if you haven't noticed, I am applying this principle to our conversation as well . . . Continue!

Touché! And we agree! You approve of Hinduism's multiplicity and give me the green light to follow its golden thread, and, perhaps incorporate it in my concluding view of the universe. However, the human side you consider illogical and not deserving your attention. But that's exactly it: the human aspect is what concerns us most, as all these philosophizings will eventually impact our future, and we want to know, what good or bad abstract thinkers, and their potential transplants/disciples have done and will do to mankind with their distorted truth! On an earthly level, we have no choice but to conclude that history's most ancient, recorded prophets, Brahma, Shiva and Vishnu, though profoundly sagacious and influential, have failed to transmit their message with sufficient force and clarity, for their teachings to remain unadulterated in the hands of lesser but more unscrupulous genius. As a consequence the prophetic pronouncements and moralizations have undergone extensive interpretations, and have become the tools of a powerful class (the usual 1 percent), which, even today, holds sway in the Hindu world. The exclusive, empire-building philosophy of this class, the brahmins, has succeeded in bringing about a relatively obedient society but failed miserably in achieving the social and economic salvation of the masses, while preaching spiritual salvation.

It appears that it is characteristic of all metaphysical philosophies to try to influence the few rather than the many. Individual salvation receives great emphasis, but the salvation of humanity is too large a task to tackle. But why, at all, is salvation (whatever it may be) the main "aim" of the individual? Are we so afraid of death that we do not dare to face ourselves and life here on Earth? Cannot we assume, as Hinduism teaches, that "life" is the result of a "recycling" process, starting with an act of simple and pleasurable pro-genesis? When the male sperm hits the female egg they both carry four characteristic attributes: (i) a genetic imprint, (ii) an instruction for growth, (iii) a memory trace of the ancestral line, and (iv) a nuclear form of the "soul," the animate essence of man. All these are subjected to growth and refinement, corresponding to their own imprint. In this combination of physical and spiritual micro-infinities, which, at this time, is beyond our comprehension, the manufacture of a human being takes place.

God's role is this manufacturing process? To provide and manipulate the basic building blocks at the micro-infinity level, where, by all appearances, the Divine Will operates. Just because we cannot define it this time, and can only postulate that micro-infinities may exist, it does not mean that we will not understand them in the future. A century ago we did not have particle accelerators, and thought that electrons were the smallest units of matter. Then came neutrons and now quarks. The miniaturization is not over yet, and will not be over before the unit of spirituality is found, at, what I called the micro-infinity level, or something like that.

The tolerant Hindu would cherish these wild speculations. However, we have to wind-up this chapter on Brahma by admitting that he gave us a tiny light at the end of the tunnel. The problem is that his henchmen have filled the tunnel with some ingenious traps, including hells, devils, demons, monads, demiurgos, and a host of other spirits. Let us see what Buddhism did to these. Or rather, what Buddha did as a prophet.

IX

Buddha—560–480 B.C.

In the millennium preceding Jesus, Buddha was the second major prophet. He expressed almost agnostic thoughts, when he said that the human mind is incapable of reaching the boundary of space, or explaining the beginning of time, or defining a final causality which lacks a cause. These profound thoughts were not strange to Hinduism either, but, as we saw, the brahmins made sure that the message got lost on everyone but themselves while the uninitiated kept on wallowing in ritualistic idiocies. Buddha rejected most rituals and taught the principles of "maitri," which could be best described as an attitude of goodwill, despite the fact that he neither believed in the possibility of eternal peace, nor in the lasting reign of goodness on earth. Therefore, he only preached to his chosen disciples, and ignored wider audiences. Yet his influence was profound, perhaps because "judgment" and "punishment" were foreign to his philosophy. In any case, eternity was not his subject. But he had to make some reference to the afterlife. Therefore to bridge the gap between the two sides of the point of "death" (which long puzzled other thinkers), he invented a convoluted Nirvana, the extinction of individuality and absorption into the supreme spirit of the self as the highest goal of man. In other words, the animate essence of man must enter into limbo, through complete control, negation and even annihilation of all human emotions, attributes and desires already in this life, to reach perfection. This he might carry over into the afterlife side of Nirvana where everything that once was a human being, is now in a state of blissful rest, in nonexistence and decay.

I used bridge and limbo to describe Buddha's description of the "soul-in-transition" between the self-denial side of Nirvana before death, and the eternal side of Nirvana after death. The first bridgehead could be described as a state of inactive, though cognitive vegetation, purposelessly preparing for death and therefore hardly worth living. In this "limbo" you walk over the bridge of death, into another "limbo," the second bridgehead, now in the state of suspended animation, and enter the eternal side of Nirvana, the extinction side (and this is the Sanskrit meaning of the word). This eventually brings you to "salvation" through complete absorption into the spiritual universe. Almost the end of the story.

If you achieved perfection while alive, and can get in (trance-like contemplation) and out (reverse-communication) of Nirvana at will, then you need not die. But you will die, because the fundamental processes of life are destructive. If you could take this perfection with you (and there is neither guarantee, nor proof to that effect) to the other side, in the form of an immortal soul, or energy unit, or something like that, then you could be reborn, and reappear on earth as another Buddha. If you entered Nirvana without perfection, you will disappear without a trace. Rather an elitist idea.

As the explanation of the state of Nirvana is full of negativism, and is contradictory too; this part of Buddha's teaching must be of necessity obscure. In time this obscurity has become contagious and has degraded Buddhism to the level where it is practiced today: to the repetition of mantras; to the veneration of demigods through a variety of offerings; and to the same cross-fertilized view of man's place in the universe as Hinduism. This means that Buddhism has also achieved its own impasse. Nice try. Nirvana.

As Buddha left no records of his teachings, the earliest writings about his philosophy originated about 200 years after his death. With painstaking analysis Buddha researchers have peeled away the barnacles which later followers stuck to his teachings, and concluded that the following may be considered the essence of what he professed.

1. a philosophy of the critical, thinking mind;
2. a cosmological theory which ignores the origin, destination and termination of the universe;
3. an agnostic concept of godhood: the existence of an eternal, overriding substance cannot be comprehended by the human mind, therefore it should be ignored;
4. a cheerful acceptance of the world as it is;
5. a need for the concentration of the individual's efforts to attain perfection, in the state of Nirvana;
6. a definition of Nirvana as the opposite of "existence" in the sensual sense. Only in Nirvana will the intellectual part of our "being" find rest;
7. a belief in the transitory nature and ultimate meaninglessness of life on earth;
8. a feeling of obligation therefore, to shake the shackles of this existence, abandon human attributes, and concentrate on achieving spiritual freedom, "salvation," in Nirvana;
9. a nihilistic undertone in the composition of Nirvana, which stems from the futility of life on earth;
10. an elitist philosophy regarding the attainability of Nirvana: while it is a desirable state to be in, only a few will reach it;
11. only the highest level of perfection will give salvation, i.e. Buddhahood, to do continued teaching (via specific reincarnation);
12. general reincarnation is contrary to the concept of Nirvana: the animate essence of the imperfect will be absorbed in the "Dharma" of the world. Yet reincarnation is an essential part of the ancient Buddhist formula of

"causal interdependency." To my mind this contradiction/controversy is not resolved, only dogmatically stated in the formula above. Buddhism's division into the Mahayana and Hinayana does not help either.

The genius of Buddha was that despite his nihilistic philosophy he was able to develop an unshakeable serenity. His statues reflect this serenity, which emanated from a balanced countenance, an unruffled civility, a noble upbringing, and a positivistic attitude. He did not burden his followers with either the inscrutable past, or with the even more inscrutable future, but emphasied the importance of a moral life. Because of his agnosticism he did not take us any closer to a "cosmological truth" than Hinduism, as he ignored both theism and pantheism. Yet, he has improved on Hinduism by rejecting its rituals, the caste system, Vedas and brahmins.

What was left then in this "export form of Hinduism?" The Dharma, the Karma, the reincarnation, and the salvation? The Dharma (in its many meanings) or the "law of the universe," exercised by a universal-life-force, is a poorly defined substitute for cosmic godhood, yet it touches on the immanent nature of the non-material world. Nevertheless, the might of this substitute is such that it has power over the gods, degrading them to second class citizens in "heaven." Or is it in Nirvana?

The Karma is a combination of inherent fate and deed-related fate, the latter providing you with "brownie points," for your future lives. You could call this belief a precursor of predestination. Otherwise you can read into it whatever you like, except logic. Reincarnation, via the transmigration of the "soul," is wishful thinking to attain "eternal" life. It may or may not be part of sansara, the cyclic nature of the universe, but it is so shrouded in "conditions" and "mysteries," that, if it stems from a feeling of futility of this life of ours, then it can be considered a panacea for a harsh existence on earth. The motto is: do good things while alive, so that you can be reborn into a higher social "stratum," or caste. Whoever invented this concept (Brahma?) knew human nature well, and realized that without some "hope" life is pretty bleak, and promised mankind, that they can become "Avatar"-s, i.e. new descendants of their own exalted selves by (re)incarnation.

Why anyone wants to live twice (or more) without possessing the experience, and memory, of a previous life is a mystery. Salvation is either an alternative to reincarnation, or an end in itself. The concept was manufactured for the same reason: to mollify those who are either easy to influence, or stupid, but under some circumstances could rebel. The motto is: behave and your god will embrace you to his bosom. If not, you go to hell.

The need for spiritual opiates became clear early in the game, and was played out to the hilt. Fear was not quite enough: hope of salvation that is the promise of elevating the individual from earthly bondage to heavenly bliss has increased productivity, and pacified many. But what is this bliss, and who should receive the blessing? The answer was never made quite uniform. It was the obscurity of the concept that made it intriguing and at the same time palatable to the uninitiated. If I can be "saved" from damnation in the afterlife and granted eternal happiness, I get my due reward. The devil has been neutered. Such an oversimplified tenet, no matter how "entertaining" it may look, could not prevail without interpretation, controversy and transformation. It may have given serene contentment to the pious, but it could not escape from the straight-jacket of contradiction which the churchmen were anxious to hide.

The appearance is that no matter how lofty an idea one man's divine spark can develop, in another man's hand it will be screwed up and will hardly resemble the original thought. The "ens realissimum" the most realistic concept of existence will be lost, in platitudes and ceremonies. "Circus Maximus." What say my lord?

You are amazed that I did not do a better job with these select specimens of your companions on earth. If I did, you would be crit-

icizing me for repeating myself and creating something in my own "image" (to use your terminology). I thought you understood that there is no absolute, and the moment you admit relativity as an inevitable part of the make-up of the universe, you admit the possibility of alternatives as well. Your species' development is a good example of that. Your theory of natural selection and the survival of the fittest, you could call an "alternative relativism" as it stipulates that an experimental unit either survives, or dies out, or in some instances mutates. These alternatives take place in "relation" to the given environments, which, in themselves, are subject to the "rules" of relativism. Your Darwin fellow used his divine spark well, and was even more influential than your Buddha, or Jesus, but, as he was going against the petrified church (intellectually speaking), he could not be declared a prophet or a saint. (Forget the aphorism!) Earlier I told you that you need a thousand generations, figuratively speaking, to start to comprehend my being, and our "relation." The great thinkers you are tearing to pieces all had some brilliant insight into what you called the "transcendent," or the "metaphysical." You tell me that you have embarked on analyzing your "world," and examining the concepts which were developed before you, also in the light of recent achievements, in what you call "science." If so, then it is your job to crystallize the thoughts of your "genius" forebears, to lead you to your own theories. Don't worry, you will be followed by many others, who will praise, criticize and improve on what you put to paper. And remember, you and those others after you are also parts of my experiments. Therefore, to fulfill your Karma, you have to continue to search. . . .

Interesting and encouraging advice. At the same time it sounds like putting a question to my own divine spark: what is the essence of the messianic message put forward by the prophets? (We have to put Brahma and Buddha in the same basket in this regard.) How could they attract such a huge following and how could they deprive this following of its critical genius?

Love it cannot be; fear has a lot to do with it; envy is too shallow an emotion; and happiness is counterproductive to organization.

Perhaps it is the sublimation of hate, rebellion and revenge. The world around him often frightens man. Therefore, if someone tells him that through rituals, prayers or meditation he can appease the fearful forces, which he does not understand, he will make a bargain with the offered philosophy and accept its outer appearances, or rules if you like, which he does understand.

All he needs now is a charismatic charlatan, who will hypnotize him into a trance-like obedience-state, making him feel that he actually had his revenge on the hated forces, does not have to rebel any more, and can live as equal, or even superior to all creations. To understand the universe, even if only partly, is not for the 99 percent. Buddha was not preaching to them either. The 1 percent will grasp some of it, but they want to live well, because benefits in the afterlife leave them cold. Yet the 1 percent are also capable of abstract thought, and some of them will be bold enough to venture into the metaphysical.

Until the last few centuries, these adventurers remained almost exclusively within the churches, trying to reconcile god's omniscience with his omnipotence and his wrath with his benevolence. Recently, however, secular thinkers and some men of science have confronted themselves with the illogical dogmas of religions, and since we hardly ever burn people at the stakes nowadays, and excommunication has become meaningless, they have developed some bold theories. Not all of these reject God, but they are certainly rejecting the "image," which the world religions are giving him.

They are trying to build a new concept of god, which should be somewhat scientific, somewhat spiritual, and in its totality still highly speculative.

That is what I am trying to do.

Brahma and Buddha left lots of questions unanswered. Obviously, their generations were unable to construct a logical cosmology, because they had to work with the material at hand. Our generations can rely on a vast treasure-house of science, penetrating deep into the galaxies and deep into the atom.

Probably very wisely, Brahma and Buddha avoided tackling the extremes of the cosmos, both in time and in space. Rather they tried to understand the world in the here and now, and define in it the way for the betterment of man. They called it salvation, but they did not push their concept entirely into the afterlife. They taught some moral principles which are valid even today.

Accept the imperfections of the world, because everything is fragile, fluid, transitory and changeable. Concentrate on your own betterment, do your duties, and subject your ego to the transcendent forces of the universe. Use your human intellect, your divine spark, because that is the best guide in life, and respect the laws of nature, which contain the world's justice.

It is a pity that Buddha had drowned this philosophy in the nihilism of the Nirvana. With this, I have exhausted Buddha. Mankind hasn't got much further either. Or perhaps a little bit: Yoga and Zen have taught us the importance of introspection, in order that we can become more tolerant where it counts most—in the thinking man's mind.

X

Moses—1250 B.C., or 1450 B.C., or 1590 B.C.

Moses, if he ever existed, preceded Buddha by about 700 to 1,000 years. Thus, his credentials are even more legend-bound than those of Buddha. Sometime after him, around 1000 B.C., the Israelites had David and then Solomon as their kings, raising their Kingdom to its apogee, and constructing the Temple. The realm split around 930 B.C. and was followed by the Babylonian captivity (about the time when Buddha and Confucius lived), which delayed but at the same time influenced the structured development of the Jewish creed. The Code of the Rabbis, the sum total of mosaic and post-mosaic teaching, appeared around 444 B.C. During this period many lesser prophets had emerged, but they could not measure up to Moses, though some of them had probably received their education and training in Egypt. What they did was to "idealize" the legends about him, and about the Jewish past. As almost a 1,000 years have elapsed between Moses' purported existence and the codification of his "laws," subsequent "additions" are explained.

Around Moses' time the Pharaohs' world was at its height. Among others, Amenhotep IV (Akhenaten) ruled with Nefertiti, taking a stab at monotheism. In the following restoration period the high priests' iron-fisted theocracy reconfirmed the demigod status of the Pharaohs, over whom only Osiris, Isis and Horus ruled. The trinity of the Nile seemed to be unshakable, in the New Kingdom.

Osiris was identified as lord of the underworld and of the dead. With his sister/wife Isis, who was goddess of fertility, he also represented the self-renewing vitality of nature: the Nile. Horus was the god of the sky, the supreme lawgiver, the ruler of a united Egypt, from whom the pharaohs descended. Theocracy, with the Pharaoh at its head, was supreme, and the civilization it created was the envy of the known world.

The only thorn in the burning bushes was the presence of the Israelites, who wanted out, because they were not wanted. Moses led them out through the "sea of reeds," and gave them the Ten Commandments, which he probably borrowed from Horus. He preached a jealous, angry, impatient, vain and vengeful god, Yahve, but a god who was exclusive to the Israelites and who made a covenant with Jacob, the father of the 12 tribes (descendants of his 12 sons), or with Ishmael if you read the Koran, by appointing them to be his chosen people. The acceptance of Yahve-worship also represented the missing glue to unify the tribes. Monotheism was on its way, assisted by the personality and "sleight of hand" of Moses, who was not shy to apply fear as a weapon either, fear of a superior being.

Moses' genius lies in the invention and carving of the Tablets, which he declared to be of divine origin. Before he came down the mountain he lit a good-sized fire and scorched his tablets in the burning bushes. He waited for a thunderstorm to confront his people. The effect was phenomenal: the Israelites swallowed what he said, because he had a large following anyhow, and because they were superstitious and Moses' charisma was overwhelming. Very likely, at that moment, the nucleus of the Jewish religion was born, nurtured by the completely unfounded tenet, that it had been invested on a chosen people. This was a new trick of the prophets, this time psychological, to compensate the Israelites for the discipline their religion, i.e., their relation to their god has demanded of them on the one hand, and to compensate them for the misfortunes that were to follow, on the other. As an illustration of what misconstrued religious ideas can do to people, and this is by no means the only example in history, the events below will show that the Jews had very little independence after Solomon's time. Yet they managed to maintain their messianic convictions to such extent that today, they act as if they had a stranglehold on the morality and the conscience of the world. And consequently the freedom to do as they please. The "promise" of chosenness, of course, is a fabrication, because if Yahve made a Covenant with Abraham or Jacob, not long after that he wiped out mankind in the Deluge: the story of the Jews should have been different: they and humanity should have got a second chance at paradise. Why didn't Yahve give equal weight to Ishmael? Weren't they both progenies of Abraham!

With this in mind, let us see what this interesting indoctrination has brought to the Jews, by describing a few historical events:

The rule of David and Solomon fulfilled Moses' dream, in a confined corner of the Levant for a short while. However, by 932 B.C., the Hebrew kingdom had split into two, though the Israeli kingdom endured till 597 B.C., when the fifty-nine-year-long Babylonian captivity started. A more moderate Persian rule followed till 332 when Alexander the Great descended on the Middle East.

After him the Syrians got involved, against whom the Maccabeans revolted and got a bloody nose. By 63 B.C., Rome was the master, and remained in the saddle till 33 A.D., enduring the rise of Christianity in the process as well. Byzantium was next in the area, till it was pushed out by Islam. The Turks ruled from about the eighth century onward until 1917 (except for the Crusades), when the British conquered the area and controlled it until Israeli independence in 1948. Hadrian gave the Israelites another bloody nose by defeating the 132–135 A.D. revolt, and accelerating the diaspora that began with the release from the Babylonian captivity.

The mass suicide in the Gaza area and later on the Masada heights, in 73 A.D., was also the "blessing" of Hebrew "chosenness," while the Middle Ages were full of pogroms and persecutions, consistent with Moses' curse. Then came the twentieth century with its "unfinished" war, followed by World War Two, when Stalin purged non-communist Jews, and "frowned" upon Jewish religious adherence, while Hitler eliminated it, together with a sizeable portion of the occupied areas' Jewry.

In the "unholy land" itself, ever since 1948, the atmosphere is a hotbed of strife because of the religious hatred, heated by both Arab and Jewish fundamentalist intransigence. Religion is the opium of the masses . . . Some opium! As most drugs, it is addictive and stultifying. The history of the Jewish religion is indeed full of subordinate relationships, and also, through the work of Jesus (who borrowed everything from it) and his followers during the first three centuries of A.D., it has become irrelevant: a fate which other religions must also face.

The conclusion of all this must be that another prophet has failed a segment of humanity, on both the short and long terms. Yet, it still must be asked: what has Moses contributed to the in-depth understanding of the universe, or of man?

The first part of the question is probably unfair, because the cosmological knowledge of thinkers of Moses' time was very limited, and metaphysical ideas could not be exposed either to open debate, or to scientific inquiry.

Regarding the second part, his understanding of the basic characteristics of man was superb, in its earthly setting. He knew that the "stick" of Yahve and the "carrot" of chosenness would work toward his goal. Fear and superiority were his weapons.

What was, then, the outcome of his severe, elitist, and exclusionist ministry?

It was negative: his anthropomorphic god has returned the compliment and confirmed Moses' "curse" on his own people, by dogmatizing the "chosenness."

To live under such delusion is an invitation to disaster. And therein lies the curse, because Jewish history is full if disasters, perpetrated by Moses, the great, counterproductive shaman, who, in the power struggle that ensued in the desert wilderness, took revenge on his enemies, and with them on this own people for disobedience. Not necessarily to god, but to himself.

Man's cosmic setting did not interest Moses, as he was just as much a despot as his god. Ruling the Israelites was his game, and he is turning in his grave on the success of his more than 3,000-year-old "spell," which has led and will lead to a series of self-destructions of his people. Moses has failed. Or succeeded: depending on your viewpoint. With this we have arrived at another cut-off point in the prophetic procession: is the measure of success of an ideology determined by its survival to the present? And is mere survival enough? Should a metaphysical stream of such antiquity not tell us something? Are the Hindus right that nothing ever will be resolved in this universe, as it just goes around like a top, repeating itself in various guises? Perhaps, we should ask you my lord: will another failure of the legacy of a prophet surprise you, or will you regard it as an intermediate state of affairs in an ongoing experiment?

But what is the meaning of so many failures? How many millions of our species will have to die before someone will emerge and come up with a realistic explanation of our existential paradoxes, and a positive program for a future development pattern of mankind? Someone who may make peace with you. Someone who will be believable on all levels.

You want me to tell you the future, especially your own species' future, and I cannot do that, because "facts" of things-to-come would require an absolutely predetermined universe, which creative-evolution did not provide for. The complexity of your divine spark is working in such a way as to generate concepts, ideas and hypotheses ever closer to infinity, on which you quite astutely touched. But your power of communication is still primitive, and your power to understand, despite some degree of sophistication, is still in its infancy. With such pre-conditions you should realize that a "solution" is not near yet. As to your perception of the Israelites, you correctly observed, that, what you could call, a psychological singularity is not conducive to a broad-minded view of the world, and, indeed, could derail one of my experiments before it would reach worthwhile results. You have also correctly observed and hinted at the fact that your species works quite well under pressure, especially if it is coupled with incentives. However, you tend to over-compensate for the discomfort which pressure creates, because your emotions take over. To use your own parable, too much steam will blow the top of a pot and scald those around it, till someone puts the lid back and fastens it, and reduces the fire.

Your third correct observation is that by metaphysical thinking, or you could call it prophetic thinking alone, you will not arrive at a realistic concept of me or my universe, or yours. You will have to invoke scientific/logical thinking as well, and give it an equal role with spiritual intuition/logic, in your struggle to "know." You have been copying my creative processes at your level, now try another level of relative perfection.

I think I can follow you my lord, but the picture is still far from complete because Moses only left us with the Ten Commandments, but did not leave us with even a speculative non-religious cosmogony. Neither did he leave us with a forward-looking and attainable secular social system. Let us see if Zarathustra will help us to work our way to a higher level of understanding.

XI

Zarathustra (Zoroaster)—630–550 B.C.

In his time a major influence, but today only a minor factor in the religious communities of the world, Zarathustra's legacy is more in what he gave to Christianity and Islam, than what he achieved with his own religion. There is no clear agreement among historic scholars, but by some accounts he lived around (oldest record) 1320 and 1200 B.C., in northwest Persia, where he was a priest. Other accounts would indicate that he preached during the 7th century B.C. In any case, his religious conversion, which came from a vision, put him in opposition to the militant, polytheistic clergy of his region and he had to flee to the east, to find asylum in the Achaemeid court.

It appears that at the beginning he was a pure monotheist: Ahura Mazda (Ormuzd), the wise lord, was his god. Later, however, he shifted into a dualistic structure, where Angra Mainyu or Ahriman represented the opposing, irreducible, ultimate evil principle, with more or less equal status. Ahriman was engaged in a 1,200-year-long battle with Ormuzd, which should have ended with Ormuzd's victory. To make matters even more complicated he introduced Mithra, who represented an intermediate "room" in Zoroastrism; Zurvan, as infinite time, and supreme being, and Saosyant a semi-divine savior. With this he adequately confused the field for later interpretation.

In preaching the worship of only one god, he had to break sharply with the Persians' previous belief in many gods. To support his ministry and to justify his vision, he is supposed to have written the Gathas, a collection of hymns, in honor of Ormuzd, who is the supreme spirit, and who is assisted by a hierarchy of subordinate spirits. This apparent monotheism, however (as mentioned above), was tainted by a parallel dualistic, and even polytheistic heaven, where Ahura Mazda, or Ormuzd, the god of creation, light and goodness, is in constant struggle against Ahriman, the spirit of evil and darkness.

Zarathustra's religious system was to be known as Mazdaism, and is set forth in the Zend Avesta, a body of oral traditions, probably not put in writing until about 400 A.D. This tradition demanded prayers five times a day, a custom which eventually crept into Islam. Zarathustra's followers taught that at the end of the 1,200-year-long battle between Ormuzd and Ahriman, a new god, Saosyant, the redeemer, the savior, will raise the dead, separate the good from the bad, and deal with them accordingly. This post-resurrection theory is obscure, hazy and infantile, as it relates the regeneration of the bones to the earth, the blood to water, the hair to vegetation, and the life-force (soul) to the fire, which when united will ascend to heaven through the magic of the Magi-s (priests).

This concocted belief in reincarnation, and post-reincarnation eternal life, which in itself was the result of cross-fertilization, from Hinduism, found its way into Christianity as well. There it became much more formalized, though not less controversial. The Trinity had to be clearly defined, the role of "God," the "Son" and the "Holy Ghost" (a not too original combination) properly outlined, judgment day made plausible, purgatory and hell believable, resurrection and salvation a positive hope, and the devil, Satan, a reality. To this end to explain these "pluralities," various synods have concocted etymologic "guidelines," dogmas, best expressed in the Nicene Creed, which, perhaps, looked even logical to a degree, except for the nature of Jesus, and the eucharist. The canonical controversy over the problem of homousion (consubstantiation) versus homoiusion (transubstantiation) would not permit the total glorification and deification of the Nazarene, not even to the measure of an "iota." In that schism Jesus' credibility as a "god incarnate" was shaken, without, however, diminishing his importance as a prophet, and as a tool for the purposes of the church.

Zarathustra also had to struggle with his monistic dualism. He realized that the irreconcilable nature of truth and untruth should not exist side-by-side in a benevolent god (there is something parallel in Judaism too). Therefore, he was almost forced to supplement his pantheon with other beings like Ahriman, etc., even if he only gave them a 1,200-year-long action plan. 1,200 years have passed, twice over, Ormuzd hasn't won yet, the world is just as rotten, as ever, and Zoroastrism has only about 100,000 followers left (Parsees). In the meantime not even the ancestors of the proverbial three wise men (of nativity stories) could have removed the superstition-rooted fear from the worshipers' soul, even if, they promised them gold, myrrh and frankincense and probably a good few "shots" of "hauma," the favorite intoxicant of the Persian religious culture. The god-induced, Magi nurtured, fear-compensation frenzy on Ormuzd's holy days has culminated in an orgy-like, hypnotic atmosphere of fire, bull sacrifice and drug-induced adoration, and of course mass hysteria. The Zoroastrian ceremonies must have been quite a show!

Irrespective of the above, Mazdaism has demanded from its followers a high level of ethics, which has remained with the Parsees to the present day and has resulted in the development of a dependable social layer, as far as work performance and personal reliability are concerned. Idealists of Zarathustra like to put the origin of their religion into the 12th century B.C. arguing that the Gathas were written in an archaic linguistic form, which prevailed well before 1000 B.C. The relation of Zarathustra to the Achaemenid court, and later to Darius, would put his prophetic activities to around 600 B.C. In this case, he must have been a close

71

contemporary of Lao-tse, Buddha, and the Jews' Babylonian captivity.

The millennium before Jesus was a fantastically fertile period of religious innovations, and certainly created a background and a lot of root-material for the emergence of Christianity. Zoroastrism had a role in it too, by emphasizing monotheism, and, while it has become a travesty of a religion as it continually made allowances for pluralistic, anthropomorphic ideas regarding the composition and operation of the extrasensory world (and its relation to our sensory world), its ethical contribution to human evolution and psyche is commendable. Its tragedy was that Alexander the Great and other armies of those times criss-crossed the Middle East, the purported cradle of civilization, decimating Zarathustra's followers, and halting a healthy development of any philosophical thought along his original tents. Zoroastrism has also failed to redeem the world, or give it a believable perspective. The appearance is that man, and consequently our great prophets have learnt from the saying:

". . . and god created man, and built into him obsolescence . . ." but translated it in practice to read: " . . and prophets created religions, and built into them obsolescence . . ."

On a cosmic scale this "built-in obsolescence" means that we and our works don't live forever. On a philosophical scale it means that we can only attain the degree of perfection in a lifetime, which does not exceed the level of our incompetence.

Zoroastrism has attained this level in its confrontation with Islam.

XII
Confucius—550–480 B.C.

Already primitive man and even animals have been known to strive toward "order." The polar bear will bite her cub if it is out of line. The alpha male wolf will subdue recalcitrant pack members. Man, in his progression to maturity (the longest among mammals), in addition to needing a kick-in-the-pants sometimes, also needs psychological crutches to make his life, if not fully understandable, at least bearable. These crutches include a feeling of belonging and being wanted, a feeling of uniqueness, a feeling of importance, a sense of cosmic purpose, a sense of the mystic, a sense of the divine, and a sense of authority. One could almost say that he needs a god to overcome an overwhelming sense of solitude and helplessness. Confucius was a man of order. However, he did not look for the regimentation of the heavens, but for a system of ideas which could govern the apparatus of the state, and through it, the behavior of the masses.

Thus, you could call him a morality philosopher rather than a religious prophet, though his influence was prophetic in the historical sense. His organizational ability has created an almost model state. His ceremonial systems survived a millennium. His ethics were exemplary. But he also had antagonists.

His main rival was Lao-tse, the sage, whose work is recorded in the "Tao te Ching," the "Book of the eternal world-law." In this book a socialistic philosophy is expounded, with a moralistic super energy, the Tao, overseeing the running of the world. This concept is similar to Buddhism's Dharma, but without the Karma. Tao is claimed to be the quintessential and universal Chinese idea, to describe the primeval forces that govern us, without, however, these forces taking up any shapes or forms.

Tao is also the energizer of the two ancient, subsidiary forces, the "Yang" (masculine, positive) and the "Yin" (feminine, negative).

Lao-tse's followers have corrupted this relatively pristine idea, by introducing quietist and mystic elements into Taoism, and have made it look more and more like a religion. Confucius fought against these tendencies, rejected the Taoist heavenly circus, and emphasized the importance of moral values, which are equally beneficial to the individual and to the state. I would call him a scientist and an agnostic. These two great minds differed in their appreciation of the philosophical reality of man in relation to the abstract, the extrasensory and the practical. Lao-tse needed a god-concept to frame man into an acceptable behavior pattern; Confucius only needed morals.

*　　*　　*

Lao-tse felt himself to be the metaphysical superior of Confucius, who, in turn, despised Taoists for their superstitious rites, meaningless celebrations and unbridled fantasies. In one thing, however, they agreed: that the cult of ancestors is the most important element in Chinese religio-moral life.

Confucius has won a limited victory and became the guiding force for the state and for society as a whole, while Taoism was supposed to give solutions to individual problems, towards the achievement of inner peace and quietude.

This can be acquired through obedience to the requirements of man's nature, in accordance with the Tao, the "Way," the basic, eternal law and principle of the universe.

The word "confusion" comes from Confucius' name, but actually it was the Taoist camp that has created convoluted theories, obscure philosophies approaching the orphic, and a phantasmagoric spirit would, which was confusing even to the initiates. However, as Confucius has become the main figure of Chinese philosophy, and even he kept a sort of a Tao (law) in his vocabulary, the lack of clarity in Lao-tse's successors was associated with him.

Popular Taoism has developed such a pantheon of godlike creatures and spirits that it borders on the ridiculous. The top three, however, should be mentioned, to support my contention that up to now no religious metaphysical system was able to avoid the pitfalls of anthropomorphism. Start with Ju Huang Sang Ti, the master of heaven, otherwise known as the Majestic Jade Emperor, followed by T'ai-Ki, the ancient beginning, the personified Tao, who in his gigantic form created the world; and then Lao-tse the deified prophet. Even Confucius was made equivalent to heavenly and earthly gods by the last Chinese emperor, in 1906!

It is difficult to say otherwise then, that Taoism has lost all its credibility regarding the cosmogony which it has developed, and therefore can be considered useless in any search for a probabilistic explanation of the metaphysical world. Confucianism, on the other hand, survived as a reform movement, emphasizing responsible action, and developing compulsory orthodoxy in Chinese political life, through an ethical system based on deep respect toward one's ancestors, devotion to family and maintaining justice and peace. Confucius himself was a man of learning who often said that his knowledge did not come from some kind of a revelation, but from extensive studies of the ancient books and customs, and from a love of history. His legacy is summarized in five so-called "canonic" books and four classic books. His humanism can be best described by his belief that man is naturally good, and in his effort to raise his whole people to a high level of morality. His success would indicate that a Taoist type, pseudo-theistic religion, no matter how purely it was conceived, will eventually degenerate itself into a quagmire of superstition and groundless mysticism, betraying its original purpose, which was the pursuit of happiness. Confucianism will prevail because it has avoided this pitfall. Confucius has maintained that a moral-philosophical system, built upon the inner value or goodness of man, with due respect to the metaphysical, or rather, to the thinking individual's self-criticism, can survive the times because it has the ability to grow in a rational manner, and is rooted in sound earthly concepts.

Isn't it ironic that history had to produce communism which has tried to eradicate both gods, religions and morals in its ideological craze to create a faithless and classless society? However, not even communism is absolutely totalitarian. It therefore carries in itself the sprouts of its own demise. Hardly a century has elapsed between Lenin's rise and Gorbachev's "glasnost." Maoism is still alive in China, but the cracks are obvious. For one, who lived through it all, it is gratifying to watch the dying phase of the age of the "proletarian experiment," communism. Religion, on the other hand, seems to be harder to kill. Man's craving for support will always try to reach up to a god, or gods, because up to now no one has been able to prove that there are no gods, and he hopes that someone could help him.

Confucius' philosophy may be resurrected one day, because the Chinese people have been steeped in the veneration of the past, which is kept alive in Taiwan, and because Confucius has taught enduring values.

Is it a failure of Confucianism, and especially the remaining influence of Taoism, that they could not stop Mao Tse-Tung's tide of slogans from winning?

Is it that, as so often in the past, one "religious" philosophy was fighting the other, neither of them really coming out on top, only replacing one servitude with another? Is it that, as the saying goes, history repeats itself: Judaism was clipped by Christianity; Christianity was clipped by Islam; Islam is being clipped by the Sunni/Shiah controversy, Confucianism has been clipped by

Communism, and now it is Communism's turn to be clipped by globalization, and by the scientific cosmogony and cosmology of the twenty-first century.

In the meantime, Confucianism is enduring under the surface, as its merit in history is that it tried to raise man up, on his hind legs, convincing him that he is strong enough to stand on his own, or stand with his fellow man, without debasing himself into repetitious, religious rituals; man-made dogmas, fear-generated worship; and without submitting his divine spark to the misguided manipulations of mesmeric Moseses.

From Confucius we can learn to draft a secular morality code.

XIII

Jesus—2 B.C. to 33 A.D.

It would be futile to dispute the greatness of Jesus of Nazareth, either as a man, or as a prophet. It would be equally futile to try to prove or disprove that he was a god. Two things, however, appear to be certain, despite some researchers' doubt:

1. that, historically, he has existed, and
2. that he was a flesh-and-blood human being.

To twenty-first-century man it is much more impressive, believable and beautiful that a fellow man, this Jesus, has been able to elevate himself through his divine spark to such heights, that, in more primitive times, other men could believe that he was a god. Why should he have had a virgin mother? Why should she have had a "miraculous," "immaculate" conception? What's wrong with the ordinary way? (It has been practiced long enough.) Weren't we "created" with sexual organs, and therefore, isn't our sexuality also of divine origin? The creator gave it to us! Think about it, and appreciate Jesus for what he was, and not, for what he wasn't.

The incredibly short one to three years of his ministry are in sharp contrast with the phenomenal impact he had on mankind. Therefore, it is hard to believe that he was not trained somewhere. Other prophets had time to evolve, lived long lives, and often reached old age. Jesus' early death however curtailed his missionary work, and actually it was Peter and especially Paul, the former

Pharisee, who spread Jesus' teaching in the Greco-Roman world. Jesus' martyrdom was the food, which nourished the acceptance of his preaching. Paul's genius and perseverance was the tool, which delivered it through his travels and formalized it in his letters to congregations of Ephesus, Corinth, etc. Actually, probably Paul and Peter were the first Christians.

Christianity, however, is a misnomer. Jesuism would be more appropriate, because "Christ" means anointed, a custom, prevailing in the ancient Middle East, to honor outstanding (religious, etc.) leaders. "Jesus the Christ" is more correct, if he was ever anointed at all, as the right to do so was in the hands of the Pharisees, who did not particularly like Jesus. The story of Jesus' life is still not an open book. The circumstances of his birth are largely fictitious and have been borrowed from Hinduism and Mazdaism, with some embellishments. His father was a Jewish "tekton" (stone-mason/carpenter), and his mother a local woman, both from Nazareth.

After Jesus, the couple had several more children, thus the virgin birth is also a fable, also borrowed from other Eastern religions. According to the New Testament Jesus has never over-emphasized his mother: it, simply, was not "fashionable" to glorify women in Judea. In spite of some pious painters' perfidy, Joseph sat on the donkey, and Mary was walking on foot. Mohammed put it well: "Jesus was Mary's son. He was only one of the many messengers (of god). Before him there were other messengers. His mother was an ordinary woman, and they both ate common food."

Evangelical sources do not say much about Jesus' youth, and even what they say is mythical. References, however, to a flight to Egypt have never resolved the time of his return. It is an intriguing possibility that as a talented, bright, young fellow, who, from an early age has shown some affinity to the Old Testament stories (his brothers were better stonemasons and carpenters than he was), has been recruited by the Egyptian clergy to undergo the rigorous training, which was a prerequisite to entering the priestly and high-priestly occupation. The culmination of the training was what could be described as a "Trial by Pyramid."

Many researchers have wondered why the pyramids did not contain mummies and other burial items. The reason, except for looting, is that burials took place mostly in the Valley of the Kings, etc. The pyramids were used for a potentially deadly game of initiation ceremony, for graduates aspiring to the various levels of priesthood.

We know that the Egyptians practiced trepanation. They also practiced a type of yoga and hypnosis as a pain control method. Through their hypnotic and self-hypnotic abilities they were able to control several bodily functions, including heart rate. The final test consisted of a three-day sojourn, buried in the center of one of the pyramids, without much air, without light, and without company. If the candidate came out alive and sane, he was suitable for the priesthood. (A similar, recent, three-day burial was in an ice block.) If the candidate died: bad luck.

Jesus passed the test almost perfectly (it was a preparation for his alleged resurrection) and received most of its benefits, but as he was an alien and a rebel, he had to return to the Dead Sea area to do something with his training and start his teachings. He was greatly assisted by John the Baptist, who paved the way for him unintentionally, having originally overshadowed him. But, when John paid with his head for refusing Salome, the daughter of Herod, things changed.

John's charisma was not lost on Jesus. When he preached the early arrival of the "kingdom of god," and he saw an opportunity to gradually step into John's place, and even outpace him by declaring that he, Jesus, was the Messiah, whom John was preaching about, and who will deliver that kingdom, he did so.

The anticipation of most people in Judea, based on these two prophets, was that some kind of a "delivery" was imminent.

The Pharisees jealously watched the events, and when Jesus

moved to Jerusalem, they arrested him and crucified him. Still on the cross, Jesus has slowed his heartbeat and consequently his blood flow, hypnotized himself into a cataleptic coma, and for all appearances looked dead. Subsequently, in accordance with his Egyptian training, he was ready to rise on the third day. He was exactly on time, and showed himself to his immediate disciples, in Emmaus. The news spread like wildfire, but the apostles guarded him carefully. Even so, Jesus' "resurrection" caused great consternation among the Pharisees. They decided to give Judas another thirty pieces of silver to get rid of him. As Jesus must have been pretty weak from the loss of blood, partly from the wound, inflicted on his right side by the spear of the Roman soldier and partly from the crucifixion nails, and also from the trauma of the events, it was relatively easy to smother him, put his body on a funeral pyre, burn it, and color the smoke of the fire with incense, in which the other apostles saw Jesus' ascent to heaven. Such is the source of legends.

With Jesus' death, not very long after that of John the Baptist, the coming of a worldly kingdom suffered a setback. To save face, that delivery gradually had to be transformed into a spiritual one. In any case, forecasts had to be pushed in the background, because early Christians were fighting for their survival, did not have time for polemics and had to take the gospels as Paul and company gave it to them. Eventually, Constantine granted freedom of Christianity, and helped the emergence of a religious patriarch in the Roman Empire.

With this, pyramid building got a good start, the top being occupied by a new concept, the pope of Rome. With astute management and strong discipline Christianity has become a huge success, both religiously and politically. Papal armies dominated the Italian peninsula, and papal might prostrated emperors.

Religious fervor started the Crusades; religious bigotry split Constantinople away from Rome; Turkish forces were attacking Christendom from Hungary, through the Balkans, and from Spain, through Africa. On top of all this, an inner rottenness set in in the Vatican. Luther, Calvin and others first tried to clean up the mess through internal reforms, but when those were unsuccessful, they split the Church further apart. A more recent test of the "divine origin" of religions came in World War Two, when none of the churches really stood up to either Hitler or Stalin. Yet, now that the storm has subsided, they are reclaiming their birthrights, and they are trying to reaffirm their idiotic dogmas. Churches (religions) have short memories. They don't want to remember that more blood was shed in the name of religions and pseudo-religious ideologies than by the Roman legions, Hannibal; Alexander the Great; Genghis Khan, Napoleon and World War I together.

Christianity's slogans, "Love your neighbors," and "Don't do unto others, what you don't want others to do unto you," have failed miserably and with them failed Jesus' teaching ministry. To quote a Chinese observer: "Nowhere was Christianity able to produce a country where true Christian values were the governing principle." The greatest curse history has visited on the Western world is dogmatic and missionary Christianity.

Despite this rather condemning conclusion, it would be futile to forecast the immediate demise of the churches, if we can not offer anything to replace their petrified cosmogony and theocracy. At the moment I have nothing more to offer than a new morality and meditation, where you might find peace. If I wanted to expound on our previous theme of the "great experimentation," I must admit that churches have created unparalleled beauty in the arts and in architecture, and also unparalleled riches for themselves. But all in all, to use a biblical expression: "You have been measured and found wanting."

Sometimes it is worth while to look at ourselves in the light of outside observers. The Chinese sage Lin-Yu-Tang has described the essential contradiction in Christian god-man relationship in the fable of the original sin.

"When Adam and Eve ate an apple from the forbidden tree of

knowledge, God became so angry that he chased them out of paradise and condemned their descendants to carry the burden of the original sin forever. But, when later, these descendants have killed his only son, he so rejoiced, that he forgave everyone!"

This rather witty statement touches on the obviously non-divine origin of the story, and also demonstrates what people would swallow from great story-tellers of the ages. At this point I should ask: how now my lord? How would you answer Lin-Yu-tang's comments regarding the original sin? And his rationale for salvation?

No!! I won't do that yet, because the misbegotten idea of the original sin, requires a little more exposure. In a fear-governed religious society the threat of damnation, hell and devils represented a powerful weapon in the hands of the clergy, any clergy.

Two questions should arise, however: (i) how could such an infantile story, like the apple on the tree of knowledge, ever attain a sort of "credibility"? And (ii) how could a succession of brilliant churchmen, like Thomas Aquinas; Francis of Assissi, Benedict, etc., not see through it and expose Christianity to arguments like those of Lin-Yu-Tang?

The answer must be that humanity has always liked unbelievable fairy tales, and that the churches have exploited the credulous nature of their fellow men, knowing well that the vast majority of scriptural stories are fabrications, amusing, annoying, and often purposeful abuses of the creativity of our accident-prone divine spark, purely invented to keep the "sheep" in line, and the churches in power.

As we were not vigilant enough to use our critical faculties, these stories have become institutionalized, and were applied already to the fetus still in the womb. Our lack of protest resulted in a largely brainwashed society, unable to withstand the accumulating effect of repetitious indoctrination on the developing individual, still on the learning curve. No wonder that these absurd stories, heard by Christian children "ad nauseam," pre-conditioned young adults to digest them almost at face value, in terms of a "subconscious determinant" regarding their uneasy feeling that they are guilty, without knowing why. Not even Jesus, whose familiarity with the Old Testament has been mentioned by several researchers, took upon himself to straighten out the story, which, with a little Freudian help, originally could have been absurdly sexual, and therefore unacceptable, of course. A young Eve has suddenly discovered the essential difference between herself and Adam, and in her curiosity scratched Adam's apple (his testicles this time), causing an erection and subsequent intercourse. Through this act they discovered the (tree of) knowledge of the pleasure of sex, and at the same time opened the door to (the tree of) eternity, by begetting children. From this, by sublimation, the writers of the Old Testament got to the apple on the tree of knowledge, missing the tree of eternity, throwing in a snake (phallus) into the works as well, for good measure.

How is this for a "counter-story"? Freud would probably approve of it, and if a segment of mankind thought that god got mad for this apparent transgression, then that segment of mankind must be mad, because the almost universally applied driving force for the continued (re)creation of life is the sexual urge, which is obviously cosmic in origin. The birds do it, the bees do it . . . etc.

There is a hitch, however, in all this. My counter-story can only have some meaning, if our young couple were "created" separately from monkeys. Perhaps Adam came first, in full sexual development, and Eve after, either in a pre-pubertal state, from which she had to mature into an ovulating female, or as a fully developed woman, immediately capable of observing their nakedness. The more you spin a story like this, the more idiotic it becomes, and forces you to return to pure and not-so-simple evolution, where sexual differentiation had to be built into living things at an early stage, because, apparently, god could not devise a way for complex organisms to replicate themselves, under fully developed conditions, and had to go back to basic cell functions, where division at the microscopic level, and specialization at the microinfinity level is still possible. From all this the conclusion must be that sexuality is divine, and original sin does not exist. Welcome to god's laboratory. But back to Jesus. In historical retrospect all arguments about his person being consubstantial with that of god, or something different, are meaningless, because cosmologically he was naive, and did not claim to have had divine revelations about the universe as such, or about his own origin.

If he was really the son of god, as he claimed, he should have been able to see the future as god planned it, and could have hinted that 2,000 years after him man will have a better understanding of the universe and of himself than in his days. Instead, he was harping on the awards of the afterlife, and the perils of hell, essentially advocating a universal death-wish. Jesus was never thinking scientifically, and made no attempt to analyze man's basic cognitive functions. If you told him that the threat of crucifixion will activate his hypothalamus to secrete a chemical called corticotrophin-releasing hormone, which will stimulate the pituitary gland, to send another hormone into the bloodstream, causing the adrenal glands to release cortisol, then he would have associated you with the devil. Yet, the adrenaline would have been flowing . . .

As he was not the son of god, he could not have known about all this. Actually he was born into an impoverished, proletarian Jewish family far from the cultural centers of the Roman Empire, in a parochial little community. He never dealt with historical, cultural, art-related or political issues, and was not familiar with other, non-local religions or philosophies. His education, apart from a possible Egyptian training, was completely Old Testament centric. His view of society was communal, and one could call him a forerunner of idealistic communism. With such a background, his success is even more remarkable.

Sociologically, he was a rebel, and was on the side of the downtrodden. That is probably why they kicked him out of the Egyptian clergy: he was arguing too much against the divinity of the Pharaoh, and against the pantheon of Pta, Ra, Amon, Osiris, Isis and Horus. He was trying to introduce Old Testament style monotheism, with which Akhenaten, Moses' teacher, had already experimented once. It was only later, when he declared himself the Messiah, and the son of god, that he transformed the Osiris, Isis, Horus trinity, into the Father, Son, Holy-Ghost triumvirate, leaving the feminine element (Isis) out of it completely, but reviving it in a mother complex.

In all likelihood Jesus realized that he had started something big. However, he never gave it a framework. He remained at the level of the Levant. His only and constant reference to the future was the coming of the kingdom of heaven. But, in that regard, he could not deliver. It was therefore up to those who came after him to realize that kingdom, in a less lofty form, in the unholy kingdom of the church.

But how about Jesus' relationship to god, the father? In the biblical concept, the supremacy of god would indicate that god had to observe his own glory first of all. This could not be done either in an "empty space," or in a purely "spirit" world: "angels" singing constant hosanna would have probably bored him. He had to create something tangible, something bold, something exiting.

Like a universe, like a human being. God became adventurous, fully knowing that when he steps out of his "absolute," spirit, invisible existence, he will have to deal with aberrations, due to the forces he has unleashed. No matter though, because eventually his "divine will" will put everything right.

Jesus learned from this lesson, and while preaching humility, declared god to be his father, assuming the self-glorification process for himself, without god ever saying that Jesus was his son. And as a son, was he at all circumcised?

When Jesus placed himself on the throne of god, he had no choice but to over-emphasize the importance of a (fictitious) life after death. With that, he has predestined the Christian church to failure, because he did not give his followers a practically achievable goal on this earth, parallel with their so-called, god-related duties. He ignored the fact that, if we are destined to multiply, then we have to work to survive.

He also ignored the probability that humanity will mature, and might question the past, the Bible, and his own teachings too. Jesus was not a visionary in terms of, say, a thousand generations. He preached a static heavenly hierarchy, in which we had better believe, or we will be "damned." He gave us "judgment day" as the ultimate resolution of the future of the "soul." Though that day may have appeared to be close in his time, 100 generations later it seems incomprehensible, meaningless and a cop-out. When the sun's energy runs out, that's the end of the earth, unless we blow ourselves up earlier, or a cosmic "accident" occurs.

In the meantime, as Jesus' religio-doctrinaire teachings have produced mainly negative results (a corrupt church, a divided humanity), a new, secularly inspired spiritual discipline must be found to replace religious morality.

The center of this search of course is again an intelligence superior to ours, but accessible to all. The proper definition of such a "force" has eluded humanity since the dawn of history. The question is: can we do better? The answer is: we should be able to, if we cultivated in ourselves that portion of "the" superior intelligence, which I called our divine spark. This tiny spark may eventually grow, to open the door to the secrets of the universe. To make it grow is our job. It cannot be adequately emphasized that our work will not be easy. With this, my lord, I give the word to you. But where should you start your comments on Christianity?

Always start at the beginning and make it simple. You are asking me about one of my experiments which is still struggling with itself, spurred on by the very few visionaries of your species within the structure, and a much greater number of critics outside of it. Both these groups have the courage to think, despite the fact that their faith has been shattered by the logical power of your new cosmologies, forcing them to reevaluate practically everything

87

that they thought of previously as "sacred." This is admittedly a difficult task and will require time, perseverance and some self-denial.

The process itself has already started, and it will be interesting to see whether Christianity, Islam, Buddhism or Confucianism will come out on top, that is to take the boldest and most comprehensive steps toward a scientific-spiritual type of thinking, which is necessary to override your preconditioned, stuck-in-the-mud egos.

As I said, you are pointing in the right direction. You are also right to observe that I do not require you to worship me: civil discussion will do. Neither do you have to fear me: now that you know that I am accessible, you can rationalize occurrences outside you, whereby they can lose their frightening aspects. You are right to try to cultivate a higher level of spirituality in yourself where communication between us is going to be more meaningful. This has been done before though. Your great mystics have often reached me, just like you, but when they thought that they did, they asked me for my help. No way! You got all the structural help you will ever get from me, when I gave you your divine spark. This of course does not mean that you cannot talk to me. On the contrary. Keep in touch and debate your thoughts with me. Keep your divine spark active.

The reason that you are still fumbling is that most of you thought that this spark is static and confined. It is neither. It is dynamic and that is its essential divinity. As you said, you can make it grow, but you can lose it too. Improve upon it because therein lies your destiny, which will formulate you, as one of my highest experiments.

I know that you wanted to ask me if these experiments are exclusive to your little planet? Of course not. But, as I told you before, you will have to find out about that by yourself.

Thank you. It looks to me like an interesting perspective is opening up, which, however, cannot be very well explored without talking about our last great prophet, Mohammed. Let us push on then.

XIV
Mohammed—570–632 A.D.

Mohammed was forty years old when he started his ministry. Jesus was thirty. Jesus operated for three years, Mohammed for twenty-two. Islam reached territorial dominance in less than a century. It took Christianity about three centuries to establish itself in the Roman Empire. They both reached their zenith around the eleventh century, and met head-on in the Crusades: another typical example of religious mass hysteria.

The Ottoman Empire, which ensued, returned the compliment (1300 to 1919) and pushed the theater of hostilities into Europe. The infamous, continental pincer-movement attacking Vienna from Hungary, and Paris from Spain, and then joining forces on the way to Rome did not materialize. Hannibal had conquered the western half of the empire, but this time Isabella of Castile proved to be a tough adversary, and eventually pushed the Moors back to Africa. With the reconquest of Budapest, the European armies have beaten the Turks back to the Balkans, but this was not a Christian war, because Christianity had already split, and was on a critical downward spiral, declining steadily, but as a result of imperialistic policies. After defeat on two fronts Islam started to decline as well.

No longer were the progenies of the prophet the rescuers, and nurturers of Greco-Roman culture, a role they filled splendidly during the dark ages of Christianity. In addition, they lost the momentum of the messianic fervor of their faith, to such an extent, that, similarly to Christianity, they could not compete with the two great mesmerizers of the twentieth century: Hitler and Stalin. Fortunately, Hitler and Stalin died and left our two "religious" religions (which claim divine revelation as their origin) to struggle on, try to reform themselves (feeding on their old and dying glory), and at the same time fight each other in different guises, keeping a wary eye on the Israelites in the Palestinian conflict.

As the process of decline is not over yet, and miracle of miracles, it may even turn around, we may just as well wait for a new Messiah. But, there does not seem to be one on the horizon. And thank goodness for that! Have we not had enough of them in history already? Could we have someone, for a change, who could look at this world with a sense of humor (even if it is irreverent humor), and with a lot of common sense? Did Jesus or Mohammed ever make people laugh?

If Jesus can be described as the great re-teller of boring, borrowed stories, then Mohammed can be described as the great synthesizer. He was certainly better educated than Jesus, traveled widely, was exposed to both Christianity, Judaism, and eastern religions, and was a leader as well as a preacher. Also very likely he was an epileptic.

Both believed in a geocentric world, cosmologically as well (the earth for them may have been still flat), man being the be-all and end-all of god's creative effort, god's actors in god's theater so to speak. (They should have been familiar with Greek dramas and Euclidean geometry.)

In this theatrical scenario there was both a beginning and an end of creation with a total stage presence of about 6,000 years. Then: curtain.

It is easy to criticize this kind of a "Weltanschauung" today, as mankind has managed to broaden its horizons, and among others, walked on the moon. But when you are boxed into a bit of a land called Judea; or another one, called Arabia, and you don't have a rocket to go up and see that this world of ours is huge, then you will be inclined to be parochial on the one hand; and to populate the realm of the stars, on the other. There you don't have to deal with facts, and the horizon is limitless.

Archaeological research has shown that by about 3000 B.C., the civilizations of Egypt, Mesopotamia, the Indus Valley, and China had been showing strong developing tendencies. If "creation" took place (in round figures) around 4000 B.C. (Luther), then humanity only had 1,000 odd years to develop racial characteristics, and spread worldwide. Genetically this seems very, very unlikely. We know that Egyptians of 5,000 years ago were very similar to our own physique, and the races have been well established as white, yellow, brown and black. It is very doubtful if god would have entered into an enterprise which is easily questionable by his most precious creation, man. One cannot imagine him putting prefabricated creatures on earth.

Thus, Jesus and Mohammed had to work with the material at hand, borrowing what they could, and inventing what they could not, thereby becoming intellectual opportunists. Mohammed had the better time of it, as he was one of the few prophets who practiced, and promised ample sexual gratification, in the company of heavenly houris, for those who died in battle, etc. Likely story. But they swallowed it.

Of Jesus' sex life we do not know much. Of Mohammed's sex life the stories are plentiful. Jesus only gave us oblique sexual norms. Mohammed changed the rules to suit his libido. But sex was a slippery subject even in those days, and therefore Jesus only promised to his disciples, that they will be drinking with him from the juice of the grape in his Father's land. Mohammed rejected intoxicating drinks. As a substitute for sex, Jesus borrowed the idea of salvation and a life after life. In his reheated stories of the Old Testament, he promised eternal bliss: an inane bunch of stultified soul-remnants reflecting an imagined heavenly light, which emanates from god's presence, creating an asinine grin on the faces of the redeemed, characteristic of imbeciles. Do you really want it?

Eternal damnation is equally absurd. Can you imagine roasting in hell forever, just because you lived like an average human being: good, bad or indifferent? What kind of a god would concoct something like this for his "own glory"? This is worse than the proverbial: man's cruelty to man, which can be pretty bad, and does not need devils to prod you with red-hot forks. So let's get rid of this apparition and ask the devil of it nicely: ". . . Dear devil! Would you (please) take off your makeup and fade away?" And take hell with you.

At the beginning I made the statement that great men either created empires or religions. Jesus and Mohammed did both, but in different ways. Mohammed unified state and religion. Jesus' followers built a religious structure which, at its peak, had enough power to declare itself superior to states and kings, and had an army to support that claim. This may have been Christianity's downfall. But even more powerful than swords was the threat of words, using excommunication and damnation, the old "fear" elements in most man-god relationships, to induce discipline in the brethren. Mohammed did not make any bones about it either, but he preferred the carrot in heaven to the stick on earth. Christianity had to dress it in pomp and unctuousness. Which one would you choose? Could it be that Mohammedanism is a reformed form of Christianity? Sacred cows!

One would hope that there are better worlds in the universe than this. Can you imagine that, when god created the cosmos, he only selected our small planet to establish life on it? If you cannot, you are not alone. Man is already scanning the heavens for signs of life, because the tremendous loneliness, which the vastness of the sky conveys to us, makes him uneasy. Also, his brain does not let him rest. And his divine spark is prodding him too.

And besides, god has advised us to search in that direction, colonize other planets, find our extraterrestrial brothers and sisters, and compare notes. The question is: will this be possible without a war? A holy war? This time on a cosmic scale. Because extraterrestrials "must" be belligerent. Mustn't they?

By now we should have learned that "war" is a senseless "occupation." Like Christianity and Islam, war also has a "split-personality." Religions have created decaying philosophical structures, and at the same time beautiful cathedrals and art. Wars created carnage and destruction beyond belief, and heroism, self sacrifice and camaraderie, which you can honor through generations. (Isn't it interesting that the spiritual created lasting material values; and the destructive has created lasting spiritual bonds?)

Perhaps monotheistic cosmology may be mistaken, as every human activity seems to have some good and some bad in it. Perhaps, and just perhaps, those who speculated that satanic forces also govern this world of ours, may have had something there. But how to explain these forces? If they are emanations from god, then god can be blamed for them. This has been said often enough. If they are primordial like god, then they are essentially competing supernatural entities, making us to endure two systems of "divine" powers, just as Zarathustra and others have stipulated in their dualistic heavenly hierarchies.

Both Mohammed and Jesus built a type of hell into their teaching, but neither of them explained adequately how the hell, their hell, would operate. How would their hell be staffed? Would they recruit fallen angels, who were punished for disobedience, yet managed to maintain their eternal existence, even to the extent that they were entrusted with "responsible," managerial jobs? Tough question, because the existence of Satan opens a huge crack in the absolute and exclusive nature of god. (Even that of a relative god.) First, he should not have created them, if he knew (omniscience) that they would be bad. Second, he should have eliminated them (omnipotence) when he realized, that he had made a mistake. But then, we would have to admit god's relativity. And we have done just that.

Many have struggled with this "duality" before me, and some came to conclude that, if two are admissible then why not three or more, making it a plurality by populating the heavens. Thus was born a hierarchy of angels, etc., to assist god and fight Satan. And here lies the absurdity of it all: if god is absolutely perfect, why would he need intermediaries, like angels, like devils? And why would a Satan need any assistance, if she is equal? No resolution, yet, so let's go back to a sort of relativistic god (in the monotheistic form), ruling himself and his own creations who, because of his and the universe's relativity, cannot create absolute beings or things, but can let relative things loose (the Big Bang) and relative beings loose (mankind) into an evolutionary continuum, where they have real choices, as well as opportunities for accidents. And therein lies the devil. There is a degree of predestination in this too, due to the limitation of that relative structure into which, and with which god has programmed all living beings.

Mohammed realized the contradiction in pluralism as well as in his own teachings. Jesus did not. Mohammed created wealth and translated it into conquests, thereby raising the standard of living and dying. Jesus also walked on earth and knew of human misery, but did not do a thing about it while he was here on earth, except preaching against the rich. Don't you think that he should have interceded with god when he took his place next to him? Why did Jesus fail us in heaven too? Because he never got any closer to the "throne" than you or others. When he died, he was absorbed into the universal life force. He had ascended to heaven.

The greatest problem with resurrection, reincarnation, and eternal life is the question: Why? Has our, or rather Christianity's and Islam's omnipotent god run out of "new" souls, to stuff into human bodies, even though the supply is infinite? Would it not be terribly boring to deal with recycled entities instead of new ones? And how would a Neanderthal man fit into the century of his reincarnation? He would run like hell.

Mohammed was not as big on the idea of reincarnation as Jesus, though he paid lip-service to it. Mohammed gave his followers a "heaven" full of "tangible" pleasures, which the common man could understand quite well, without upsetting the fabric of the Arab social order, but with cementing an enduring cohesion.

As to hell, the religious demands of Islam were so easy to follow that only very few Muslims would get there, forcing Satan to close shop, and put her devils on welfare. The Christians still have not resolved how the soul got into the newborn, whether this soul was floating in limbo waiting for (re)incarnation, or whether it was a brand new creation of god. It would be good to remind them that the Hindus are very upset that Jesus and his church did not acknowledge that the flora and the fauna of the world also have souls, and that "matter" also has properties which tie it into the "cosmic resonance." Animals and plants have "souls," programmed in the kernel, or in the cell in such a way that they can produce a rose, a tree, a fish, a lion, an ape or a human being. This is the beauty of the micro-infinity theory: practically everything is possible at that level, and if god wanted to experiment with dinosaurs, all he had to do was to define the evolutionary journey that will lead to dinosaurs, and make the spiritual, master-building blocks obey his will.

These would assemble and put the physical master-building blocks together, make them into recombinant units, make them multiply, make them consequently grow, instructing the initially sub-microscopic, and later microscopic pieces where to go and what to do, while remaining with the "product." (Astral bodies?)

We know that genes carry instructions to perform, or help to perform specific tasks. But who, or what instructs genes? One could venture to say that it is the self-combinative power of the spiritual micro infinitic units that do the job, acting on god's command, as they are part of god. At that level, not only the desired form can be determined, but the future developmental and mutational possibilities that may, or should arise, in order to arrive at higher and higher "products," can be programmed, in such a way, that these "products," on a very limited planet, can also feed themselves and reproduce themselves. And of course, they can create an environment which will produce "food," "air," and "water." Quite a task. It would be a fair question to ask: why can we not observe significant mutations today, except in the world of microbes? Why is nature not producing new species under our very eyes? The answer is not simple, though it is probably related to time. Genetic mishaps frequently occur today, too, and they are being carefully studied. But they are the exceptions, and generally not inherited. Species mutation took millions of years, while we only have been on the scene a few thousand, as quasi homo sapiens. Give it time. Today, we should be happy that our genius, inspired by our divine spark, was brilliant enough to detect an evolutionary process in our past, and, at last, courageous enough to reject the fable of an adamistic creation.

While on the subject of creation, the Christian and Islamic stories are equally imbecile, except that in the Koran Adam is forgiven, and the general tone of the suras is much more practical than that of the New and Old Testaments. An outside observer once remarked that Mohammed appealed to Arab sexuality in the interest of winning wars, and made killing others his priority to build an empire, while Jesus wanted to bring about the kingdom of heaven by having killed himself. Mohammed, very astutely, chose his methods and means to achieve victory on earth. Jesus chose his ways to find victory in heaven and glory in defeat. They both got their wish.

The phenomenal success of the Islamic empire threatened Christendom. Ottoman armies had reached Tour et Poitier in France, and were knocking on the gates of Vienna, when partly internal strife and partly the lengths of supply lines caused a gradual retreat. It is a pity that Islam split into "Sunni" and "Shiah" sections, which caused meaningless arguments and bloody conflicts, instead of joining forces and trying to search further into the nature of the universe and god. Not to speak of the impact on the balance of power in the Middle East, and the potential for peace there.

Mohammed has been called lots of names, but nobody has ever called him impractical. From his approach to sex and polygamy, to the more abstract and obscure points of his Koran, he was the holder of the Islamic "truth." He never separated his followers' duties to Allah from those to the greater Arab community. He dealt with real life and in a more enlightened age he would probably have become a Confucian. Whether he believed in his own "visions," we don't know. But they were very useful, as he certainly believed in his dreams of power, destiny and glory.

Religion, that is an abstract, though understandable metaphysical framework, was only the means to him to achieve Arab cohesion, helped by his charismatic self, filling a vacuum. Napoleon had built an army on the ashes of the French revolution, by applying aristocratic discipline. Mohammed built an equally disciplined empire with plenty of attraction in heaven, on the ashes of polytheism, which did not make sense anyhow. His genius was to recognize Christianity's success with monotheism (which was built on a discredited other monotheism, Judaism). He realized that it was controlled through unquestioning faith, with a "little" help from fear of punishment. Nevertheless he learnt from both Christianity and Judaism, favoring the latter. He also recognized that the reason that Christianity failed to build a dynamic, Islamic type unified empire was that it essentially separated the church from the state, and therefore the two could not become a permanent single force. He further recognized that the establishment of a powerful clergy, to interpret and execute his message, was not the way to persuade independent-minded Arab tribes to follow him. He created a symbol: that was the Kaaba, a black meteorite (a pretty pagan one at that). He needed a god, that was Allah, and he needed a messenger of Allah, and that was himself, the prophet.

The resurgence of Islam's dynamic fundamentalism is one of

the unexplained phenomena of our times. Or is it also part of Moses' curse?

Islam considers itself the spiritual descendent of Abraham. But so do Christianity and Judaism as well. Isn't there a chance in this common heritage for peace and understanding? I think there is. Except for the "chosenness" . . .

In trying to answer these dilemmas I will ask some questions, in the spirit of a potential, secular morality, but with god as a guiding force, and answer them.

* * *

With this chapter my book at the seven great prophets of history is completed. What follows the Questions and Answers section is a summary of the perceived legacy of the prophets; some closing words; and a suggested morality code for the twenty-first century.

Read on.

Questions and Answers

There Is a God

1. In this part the existence of a superior being or force, a creator-maintainer of the universe, in familiar terms a god, is not questioned.

On the contrary. It is categorically stated that there is a god. It is the nature of this god, that is being scrutinized, as examining him through the eyes of seven major prophets of our history, and in the light of twenty-first-century knowledge, it is not felt that all questions have been answered by the mere "ex-cathedra" pronouncement that there is a god. The "sine qua non" of intellectual inquiry is, that it cannot, or at least should not, end in a statement of "faith"! Thus, god must be put to logical analysis, in order that a confirmation of the nature of his existence can be arrived at. Only then, when all or at least most questions one can think of have been asked, and most of them, or at least the majority of them can be answered, will we be in a position to theorize intelligently. Is this a self-serving process? Not necessarily, because we might end up in a impasse.

2. The first question to ask is this: what is god? Is he pure energy or does he have other attributes as well?

According to statements which I put in god's mouth, he is:

—an all-permeating force, too complex for humans to fully understand;

—an all-permeating intellect, inseparable from the force;

—a being without image, without limit, but with a presence;

—a being contemporary with creation, a being of space-time;

—a being who may have been self-released/renewed with the "Big Bang";

—a being who is the creator, and the creator of the creator . . . ;

—a being of logic without feelings or emotions;

—a being whose purpose is experimentation, and whose work is unfinished;

—a being who uses us as (probably) the peak of his experiments;

—a being who acknowledges kinship with us, and one we don't have to fear;

—a being we can talk to, and don't have to worship;

—a being we can respect, but don't have to love.

3. The next question is about omnipotence, omniscience and benevolence.

For the purpose of examining god's "character" I have to accept these adjectives as "absolute," at first.

If god is omnipotent, then he must be the only god in the cosmos: he has eliminated all opposition, if there was any.

If god is omniscient, then there is no need for experimentation because he would know the outcome of any of his ideas and plans or actions and experiments in advance.

If god is benevolent then he should have emotions, and should look after us.

But:

By all evidence and appearances he is not omnipotent, consequently he is "relative" and therefore the universe he has created is also "relative." However, he is potent enough within the boundaries of the universe he has created.

As he is experimenting with both the universe and with us, he cannot be omniscient. Nevertheless his knowledge is most impressive, and a constant source of learning for us, through our kinship.

It is one of the marvels of his inscrutable ways how he manages to make sense out of the huge, information "traffic jam" (both input and output), which he must deal with if he wants to be omniscient.

As he is a being of logic without emotions, his dictionary should not contain the concept of benevolence. Or, are there cracks appearing in this absolute too? Can we help? We have too much emotions, anyhow.

4. If observable manifestations of this being are "relative" to a fixed point in the universe, let us say to time, and seem to obey certain rules in that context, yet can accommodate exceptions, accidents and contradictions, where is the limit of this relativity and how do we fit into it?

Notwithstanding the third point above, the concept of divinity should correspond to the concept of the absolute. But absolutes are not observable in the universe. Therefore, beings, events, and futures must have been at least partially pre-conditioned at one time or another, resulting in only partially conceivable "truths" to cover our existence and the workings of our surroundings.

These truths are actually, what we are looking for. Their relativity is one of our hopes that we will ever find them. However, the expression "relativity" implies comparison with something, in this case with the absolute, with the unconditional, i.e. with something that actually does not exist. Therefore, if you want to define the limit of "relativity," then, because of the vastness of the universe, you have to treat it like an absolute. What a paradox!

For practical purposes we can postulate god's relativity,

though it is still beyond our full comprehension. It makes it possible for us, however, to try to access him, understand him better, and search for his emotional side, which, at the moment, is extremely well hidden. The more one thinks of it, the more one must wonder how a supposedly pure logical being, who, by the simple rules of logic should say: I have created something, I had better examine and analyze what my creation is up to, especially, if I, as a creator, have given him the opportunity to develop emotions. Further, when studying these emotions, I should weigh it if they contain "values," and if so, should they affect me? Let us hope that god has preempted us in this.

Now, if we assume that the beauty of god's relativity lies in his ability to move with the expanding universe, and consequently adjust, and change, and even learn, then by logical conclusion we can venture the statement that he might be willing to accept our feedback, and embrace emotions. I don't think that his spirituality would suffer in the process. Or, his inscrutability.

Thus, in this infinite relativity we might have a tiny niche, which we can expand with further dialogue. After all, we are not only actors on the stage of god's laboratory, but also observers and movers, even if at the moment we only move the props, on a very small scale. As to the limit of this sphere of inquiry, in our terms, it is obviously infinite, except for the curvature of the universe. This, however, need not worry us for the next thousand generations, though we, mankind, we are going to probe its boundaries. My feeling is that, with today's speed, scientific thinking could get results sooner than philosophical thinking. But if metaphysical theories get off their petrified, religious base and join forces with the hypotheses which will be built on the foundations of quantum mechanics, etc., then the process could be accelerated, and we could achieve godhead sooner.

Our place in the events to come can be only appreciated, if we look at ourselves not only as individuals, but as links in an evolutionary chain, a chain of relative eternity, to which new links will be added with new knowledge, superseding old ones, in our relentless quest to approach god.

A fantastically beautiful path lies ahead. I hope, we will not blow up ourselves before the task is completed. In this respect, we might need god.

5. We accept that the universe is real and tangible, we are real and tangible and god is real but intangible. Is however our sense of reality also "relative" to the type of perception-ability, which we possess? How can we contribute to all these "realities"? And are we really "unique" in the universe?

Until we make contact with intelligent, extraterrestrial life forms, we, mankind, are the cognitive center of the cosmos, and the only ones who can intellectualize about it. God placed us here (evolved us to this level), to do just that, because he realized that the animal, etc., world is beautiful, but without someone to conceptualize it, it is a bore. He took the risk that due to our imperfect psychological makeup we might turn against him, or want to become equal to him.

He would probably regret the first, and would apply the appropriate retributions. However, he may welcome the second, because then he could declare this particular experiment of his a success.

Thus, our role is relatively simple: strive for an ever-higher level of perfection, by cultivating that divine spark which will help you to increase knowledge, deepen spirituality, and develop an introspective morality, on a non-dogmatic, non-religious basis. This will not be easy without some compulsion. Therefore the power of prophetic persuasion (or a whip) may be needed to get through the protective crust of the material world, behind which the allures, promises, glamour, power, money, position and other ego-boosting attributes of human society are hiding, or boasting.

This could be just too big a task to manage for today's "material girl."

The phenomenal attraction of wealth, and the envy that it creates in those who cannot attain it, may lead the world's peoples into an ultimate class-struggle, divesting them of any traces of their divinity and humanity too. Dissatisfaction creates strange bedfellows, and the availability of instant communication could lead to the destruction of the world-wide web, and with it the structure which might enable us to reach higher levels of perfection. Our uniqueness in all this? It certainly exists in our galaxy, but is elusive in the universal context, and may also be hidden in god's remarks, regarding our progress in a thousand generations.

6. How can we explain the process, which we call "history" (in a broader sense), without referring to the "sacred" texts of the past?

Now that we are certain that the story of mankind is much older than the 5,960 years calculated by Luther and others (Adam's purported birthdate); now that we are certain that evolution is an anthropological fact; and now that we have stipulated that evolution and creation are not mutually exclusive if reduced to the micro-infinity level, we can abandon a religious approach to the explanation of our origin and destiny. (Faith need not be touched, till it remains within the psychological boundaries of the individual, and does not get "organized.")

The theory of evolution is not an offense to god. It can fit in very well with his relativity, with his goals, and with his "modus operandi." Once we are prepared to accept the possibility of creative/evolution, and trace god's handiwork through history, the magnificence of the process becomes "absolutely" astounding. We do not need "six-day-wonders"; a few billion years will suffice. The Bible's timetable is "passé," its stories are stale, but its moral and historical values are undeniable.

Throughout history the concept of god has not been static. It took some time for Mediterranean mankind in the cradle of civilization, and elsewhere, to develop the religions of divine revelation, and to arrive at monotheism. Or, like the Eastern "religions," to develop the idea of the "Dharma," the eternal and governing role of the universe, in a perpetually rotating cosmos.

The essence of both processes is the "pantha rei," the continuous movement and expansion of the universe, and that includes thought, to fulfill god's purpose. Or the rules of the "Dharma." Why could we not call "Dharma" god? Or the "Tao" for that matter?

History would then go full circle. We can certainly learn from the past.

7. Is the statement that the universe is a "divine laboratory" supportable, and that our destiny in it is to emulate the divine process?

A place for experimentation is a place for adventure. The adventure of the universe is truly divine. To fill "infinite space," with an infinitely expanding universe, is also a truly divine task. Can you imagine infinite space, or call it the "macro-infinity" of the world, in its timeless, not yet ordained condition, full of random energies, waiting for a god to organize them, so that they can become the basic building blocks of his intended universe, which then he can put in his laboratory, to see what can be done with them?

God accepted the challenge, considered the universe, or the macro-infinitic space, if you like, as his workshop, and started a monumental enterprise to expand into infinite time. His task is nowhere near completed yet, as even today, he is trying to perfect his most controversial creation, man.

Or, rather, giving man the task, and some of the tools, to try to do the job, to perfect himself.

Can you now feel your place and importance in this corner of the universe? And, perhaps, elsewhere too? Don't you think that we have to continue to probe? To imitate god?

8. If we are largely left to our own devices, how can we improve ourselves in our quest to achieve godhood? And what should be the guiding principle in our further "evolution"?

Historically, the production of a "genius" has been accidental. When emulating god, man, in his laboratory, will have to consciously produce exceptional human beings, with exceptional brains, by selective breeding, cloning, genetic engineering, computer symbiosis, and any other, yet to be discovered ways.

Man will be criticized by other man who might say that these processes are not "natural." But if you consider that the human mind is the result of "natural" evolution, selection and development, then those ideas will not look so strange, on the contrary, they will be accepted as the outcome of a natural property of man, thinking.

By thinking, we also produce safeguards, to operate our laboratory in both a logical and ethical manner. This safeguard is morality. Religious morality has failed us when dogmatic thinking, greed, and meaningless rituals have caused faith to slide into a quagmire of corruption.

We must develop a new morality, upon which we can base the structure of "society." This morality, in turn, will have to be built on the inner values of man, which have been implanted in us with our divine spark. These values will guide us in our quest to achieve godhood. They can be accessed through meditation.

The realization of a universal, humane morality "code" in the secular context should be the primary goal in the next steps of our progression, toward an improved "state" of mind. This code should not have to be worshipped, just observed. Confucius and Buddha have gone a long way in this regard.

9. If we are really left to our own devices, i.e., our divine spark is the only thing that we will ever get from god, can we pressure him in spite of this to reconsider? Can we appeal to his logic to analyze our innermost illogic? Can we count at all on god's help in the future? Can we influence god at all? Could we dress emotions in a logical overcoat, can we coax a smile on god's "face," which could help relieve our uncertainties and loneliness in our often mentioned quest for knowledge?

Our "first encounter" resulted in a series of polemics, in which I have questioned god; attacked god; criticized god; but only occasionally praised god, or acknowledged his greatness.

I tried to demonstrate that we can talk to god. Perhaps we can even convince him to entertain other then purely logical "things" or "concepts" like peace, love, etc. (I hardly dare to write down emotions, because they are so terribly human . . .).

He can you know! But first we may have to be on the way to maximize our own divine spark, to show god that we are serious. Then we might be able to convince him of other things as well, namely that he could help if he wanted to, and communicate with us more in-depth, if he wanted to. Alternatively, he could enhance our divine spark to accelerate its access to godhood.

In any case, all this may have to develop into a race: shall we be able to convince god first; or shall we be able to attain godhead first? In the first case we would have achieved something unbelievably great, and relax a little. In the second case, we will be able to help ourselves: another remarkable achievement. But the second state of affairs could be a "few" generations away, and human population is growing at an alarming rate.

We are talking of pollution and the damage which pollution

can do to our planet. However, the only real pollution, which we hardly ever deal with, is overpopulation. In this regard we are nowhere near the point, when we could move masses of people to other planets. Therefore we will have to think hard, to keep our emotions in "balance," or, in our struggle for "Lebensraum," we might create catastrophic conflicts.

The measures we may have to take to resolve these conflicts will not be popular. Our new morality will be severely tested when we have to deal earnestly with eugenics, euthanasia and compulsory family size, and, of course, genetic engineering. If it continues to grow at today's rate the population of the earth will double in about 70 years to 12 billion. How will our divine spark deal with that? How will god's laboratory, and ours for that matter, be influenced by it? I can imagine and others have foreseen some raw nerves, strained emotions, and revolution-like movements, culminating in suppressive, pseudo-totalitarian systems: the Orwellian phenomenon.

If we cannot convince god shortly that emotions are a volatile and potentially explosive part of human psyche, then we have to accelerate the achievement of our own divinity, or apply force. Something should be done about our emotions, preferably via education, otherwise, a spark, which is not divine, might blow up the works, and we may have to start from scratch one day, if at all. (For those who survive, some of us may become the "extraterrestrials" who teach them how to use the plow! . . .)

Communication is extremely important at all levels, even if it is only an imaginary one, like this one. While communicating, we have hope of resolving differences. God's advice would be similar on this subject: we should learn to control our emotions through logic, then god might consider accepting emotion as part of his divinity. However, a completely emotionless world would be extremely dull. Some emotions, like compassion, love, etc., we should retain in our vocabulary, as part of the new morality, which we should try to develop. This morality would dictate that those who are "more equal" than the others, assume a degree of responsibility for the 99 percent. Altruism is not an unintelligent concept, after all we are all highly interdependent, and cannot live in an ivory tower long.

We were talking of communication, emphasizing its importance in the ultimate god-man relationship. But it is equally important, as we have seen above, in a man-to-man relationship, especially today, when, through television, radio, newsprint, telephone and its derivatives, nobody is really isolated from the events of our world. In this century the average man is very much better informed than his ancestor of, say, a hundred years ago. Inevitably, this fact broadens man's horizons. At the same time communication acts as a social "equalizer." However, it has not acted yet as a spiritual or moral guide to the masses, because no one could find "sponsors" for purely moralistic programming, as no one has discovered it yet, how to make money out of it.

Television ministries are numerous, but they are still chewing on the old cud, and preaching a god whom we have to fear, even if he is merciful. The individual is not encouraged to practice his philosophy, his faith, his own way, because then there would be no need for churches, and, consequently, there would be no income for the leaders.

These leaders are still fooling their followers with the pleasure/pain alternatives of afterlife. They still cannot come to grips with the fact that it is good to live, here and now, and that this is the only life they and we are ever going to get. Life is beautiful, and can be made even more beautiful if we rid it of religious nonsense, and trust our own, personal faith and divine spark. We do not need prophets, we are allowed to talk to god directly.

True, millennia of indoctrination are not easy to overcome. But with today's knowledge at hand, we should be able to ask these latter day shamans: "Quo vadis domine," and stop them in their tracks.

10. The impact of the prophets.

God admonished me for being too hard on the prophets, whom I selected for closer examination. His argument was that I should "blame" those, who later "interpreted" the prophets, and twisted their teaching out of all recognition.

I tend to disagree, because, had the prophets supported their gospels with airtight arguments, logic and evidence, then it would have been extremely difficult to misrepresent them. As it is, their stories were fables, upon which more fables were built, till we had the good sense of asking some very pertinent questions. Thus we have to get back to the source of those religious ideas, which governed quite a portion of mankind for a quite a while. This source was the prophets. To a very large extent they are the cause of our dilemma.

Where do we stand now? It appears that we can conclude that mankind, after a very interesting post-evolutionary history, is still not much further psychologically, regarding value-judgment, than his 7,000-year-old ancestors, inasmuch as he is still unable to believe in himself, and believe that he can stand on his own feet. He does not need heavenly hierarchies to support him, he got heaven in his divine spark, his soul. He does not need the uncertainty of the "afterlife." God will take care of that. It was this uncertainty, which the prophets have exploited, to break the resistance of otherwise practical people, and make them impractical believers.

In this book I tried to show how the major prophets thought, and in many instances how their thinking was corrupted by their successors and "interpreters." Despite god's comments I have no hesitation in saying that to varying degrees all prophets were self-serving charlatans individually; catastrophic failures in bringing about social justice; and destructive influences on the unification of mankind.

The religions they and their disciples created have retarded science (e.g., Galileo), retarded medicine (e.g. no pathologic autopsy), institutionalized cruelty (e.g. the inquisitions), destroyed parts of history (e.g. Maya books and Aztec gold); and offended human intelligence (e.g. the "virgin" birth).

The worst offender is Christianity. Its history is written in injustice, intolerance and blood; its philosophy is a concoction of self-justifying dogmas; its practice is steeped in meaningless, barbaric superstition; its morality is unctuous and corrupt; its teachings are outdated; and its power has nothing to do with spirituality, but a lot to do with money. This money comes from fearful churchgoers, who try to buy their way into eternity. This money has always found its way into the coffers of the churches, even during the darkest days of history's world conflicts. The legacies of the other religions are not better: we have to live a lie if we wanted to get to the "heavens" of their gods. Questions must not be asked. Let us make some statements then.

*　　*　　*

Legacy

This brief summary of my "satirical play" (which was performed on history's stage) lists the plus and minus sides of the principal "actors," in humanity's metaphysical theater. Regretfully, the play cannot end on a positive note.

While our thespians have opened up some brilliant avenues regarding the understanding of mankind's spiritual and physical presence in the universe, they were unable to transmit their brilliance in a believable legacy, which could stand the test of time. But, of course, they were only human.

Brahma on the Plus Side.

He liberated the "soul" of the Hindu, by not developing a strictly outlined dogmatic philosophy, when defining the "Dharma," the "ancient cause" which governs the universe. No one not even the gods is excepted from under the rules of this "eternal law." He returned the faith of the individual to the individual by eliminating the clutches of regulated thinking, and permitted an unparalleled freedom of belief and freedom of expression, in regard to the explanation and understanding of the transcendent world. This freedom is the greatest gift of Hinduism to mankind. Spreading the principle of freedom could be a justification of missionary zeal.

Brahma on the Minus Side.

He incarcerated the "person" of his devotees' by developing the Hindu caste system. A rigid, exclusive social structure, not on an organized theocratic basis but ruled by a top theocracy, justified by the Vedas. In spite of this, while the spiritual freedom Hinduism grants is highly commendable, it did not manage to develop an encompassing world morality, it got stuck in the mud, and remained a Hindu system. Isolationism is a self-defeating attitude in a world which is rapidly shrinking, and the superior "caste," the brahmins, who perpetuate such inbred, social stratification and territoriality, should be doomed. And, what might kill them? Communication.

*   *   *

Moses on the Plus Side.

He left his people with a disciplinary system that stood them well for centuries and helped them withstand adversities. His ten commandments are a fair summary of enduring, behavioral norms, a type of morality. But it is still theocentrical. His god is exclusive and well suited to creating and maintaining a homogeneous society. His system was always based on strong leaders, and culminated in David and Solomon, whose autocratic religious rule presaged Islam's unified, church-state concept. After them, Moses' legacy collapsed.

Moses on the Minus Side.

He invented a vengeful monotheism, tailored to the Jewish tribes, and forced the fable of the "chosen people" idea, the "curse of Moses," on the Israelites. This "curse" still affects both the homeland of Jewry, as the Israelis are not left in peace by their Palestinian neighbors, and the Jewish diaspora, which does not show too much willingness to integrate into their adopted countries. This is understandable, because, if someone is indoctrinated from early childhood that he is a member of an "elite," a "chosen people by god," and in addition, he emphasizes his belief that he is "different" (he is circumcised), then assimilation becomes extremely difficult, if not impossible. Moses has revenged himself on the Israelites for disobeying him, but he also put a curse on the non-Israelites indirectly, as "separateness" (chosenness) implies superiority (the Jewish conspiracy), perhaps a desire to rule those who are not chosen, with the consequent tension, which historically erupted in several pogroms. Moses has really left us in a mess. His heritage in strife.

*　　*　　*

Buddha on the Plus Side.

This self-taught, aristocratic prophet did away with the Hindu caste system; dethroned the brahmins, debunked the prevailing concepts of godhead; and left open the questions of the origin of the universe; the nature of life, and the nature of death. He praised human intellect; he considered man intrinsically good; and recognized the presence of a "life-force," in all life forms; and encouraged a morality, based on intellectual conviction and not on god. He acknowledged the "Dharma," but without an eternal creator standing behind it. In summary, Buddha's philosophy could be called an agnostic morality-thought-process perhaps even a positivistic metaphysics. In this life, it is centered on the cheerful acceptance of the world as it is. Buddha is the only man/god/prophet who ever smiled. His heritage on the positive side? The rejection of the rituals as such (which his followers, however, smuggled back) and his teaching that "salvation" in the context of our existence on earth should be interpreted as living a moral life. This can be achieved individually: we do not need "intermediaries" either in a human or in a spiritual form; Buddhas are only here to show the way.

Buddha on the Minus Side.

He preached the denial of the "value" of "living" and of being alive and tried to introduce the idolization of inactivity for those who wanted to enter his rather purposeless Nirvana. He tried extreme asceticism, but when he realized that he was getting nowhere (and this is to his credit), he started eating and got fat. Immediately, life took on a more pleasant aspect.

His explanation: his teachings are for the few thinking minds of our species, those who can understand him. This, of course, would not satisfy the masses. Therefore, Buddhism begged, borrowed and stole all popular ceremonies, that were available and appeared to be attractive, from other religions, and debased spirituality to formality: perform the mantras, exercise the mudras, repeat "om mani padme hum" ad-nauseam, and paradise is yours. Question: would I study Buddha with interest? Yes, because he strove for serenity and measured self-control, but I would shy away from Buddhism as it has become too much like Christianity. What is then Buddha's heritage, on the negative side: a jovial, schizophrenic "Weltanschaung," not quite theist: not quite atheist; not quite agnostic; as if he couldn't really make up his mind. However, if nothing else, this sage knew what not to philosophize about, and kept away from both cosmogony and cosmology. But with this he disappointed many of his followers.

Zarathustra on the Plus Side.

He was a pioneer of monotheism, in the Near East metaphysical theater, whose structure of heaven has strongly influenced both Christianity and Islam. His rejection of the prevailing Persian pantheon was so courageous and unique that he had to flee from his polytheistic fellow churchmen, and develop his philosophy elsewhere. This philosophy advocated strong ethical principles, which survived as a guiding morality of the Parsees, fugitives from Muslim armies.

Zarathustra on the Minus Side.

He developed a mixture of a dualistic, even pluralistic monotheism, emphasizing morality, but celebrating with gregarious orgies. In his borrowed eschatology, death represented the gateway to judgment day, culminating in heaven or hell, after a brief resurrection.

A boringly repetitive idea. When he deviated from his pure, monotheistic concept, probably under pressure from his immediate followers, he lost his chance to inspire the masses like Mohammed and Jesus did, and consequently lost the race to Islam, in the area from Persia to India, where Mazdaism operated.

Confucius on the Plus Side.

He has institutionalized civilized human contact. His demeanor can be best described as that of a humanist. He emphasized that man's inner values enable him to stand alone in a rather strange universe, if he exercises enough introspection and obeys his propensity for morality. He also emphasized responsibility especially at the highest levels of government, which then would filter down to the masses. He developed a state apparatus, which ensured a high degree of social "justice," and an exemplary system of ethics, though these ethics were elitist and contained elaborate rituals. At the same time he produced an enduring, orderly, state-centered practical morality from which we could learn.

His legacy was the confirmation of the old Chinese respect for ancestors and their history; a love for learning; and a strong belief and advocacy, that man is naturally good. Had he lived today, he would probably be the sage of our age.

Confucius on the Minus Side.

If he had any at all, it was that he has succumbed to self-pity in the twilight of his years, and declined to participate in state affairs by retiring to teach.

This fact though is only negative in the sense of practical considerations, as his philosophy may have been recorded at that time and disseminated by his pupils. His ideas have been called boring and too etiquette-oriented by some Western philosophers, but that could have been sour grapes, as none of the Western philosophers have achieved such a profound influence on their society as Confucius, in their time.

Jesus on the Plus Side.

He gave a multitude of people the hope that our earthly existence is going to be rewarded, if we behaved well toward our fellow man as well as toward our heavenly father. This reward will be eternal life, sharing in the glory of god. He also anticipated a kingdom of heaven of sorts, on our planet or at least in Judea, bringing deliverance to his people (the descendants of Jacob), from servitude to the conquerors, and from inequality within their own society.

The latter promise was the "real sedative" as it promised complete equality before god (or rather, inequality for the rich), and thereby ensured that the lambs of god remained on a leash, creating an almost peaceful society for as long as the "system" operated.

In terms of the political aspects of Jesus' ministry, and even more so of Paul's, the impact of Christianity was so profound that it formalized the framework of society, subordinating the role of kings to Jesus' heritage, and thereby justifying their divine rights to rule. In the dark days of the Middle Ages, this could perhaps, be considered a plus, as during the great migration of peoples (Attila and company) this was, apparently, the only cohesive force that could keep alive a tenacious European identity.

These pluses, of course are very self-serving and power-centric, and survival oriented and do not indicate Jesus' success or otherwise, either as a novel religion-builder, or as a creative cosmogonist but they certainly point to the greatness of Jesus as an astute observer of human behavior and character.

117

He knew the "needs" of his people and used his stories to tell what they wanted to hear, even if sometimes he bordered on demagoguery and told recycled sermons, which were not original by any stretch of the imagination, giving them a moralizing twist. The other greatness of Jesus was his tremendous self-control (the Egyptian lesson), which enabled him to endure the tortures of the crucifixion. With his martyrdom he became the rock of his church, not Peter.

Jesus on the Minus Side.

He has left us with a religion of hypocrisy, an untenable cosmogony, a travesty of faith, an exploiting theocracy; a church of inner "deviations"; a power-hungry clergy easy to corrupt; a tenacious organization which still tries to rule by fear; and ultra-conservative heads of churches.

Originally, Jesus was a local Jewish preacher, with only an Old Testament type education (except for a "stint" in Egypt). He had little appreciation of the world outside the eastern pocket of the Mediterranean, and his goal was to rule over the 12 tribes of Israel and deliver to them the kingdom of god.

He failed the Jews: he just could not deliver. Therefore he was either a dreamer or a pathological liar. It was the apostle Paul, who did something with Christianity. But that is another story.

Mohammed on the Plus Side.

He has developed a religion of practicality and adaptability. Practicality consisted of a carpet; some water; the knowledge of the direction of Mecca; and a once-in-a-lifetime pilgrimage to the Kaaba, for the proper worship of Allah. Adaptability consisted of using sand, if water was not available, for cleansing.

These simple rules were enough to create Arab cohesion, and build a superb cultural empire, without which the rediscovery of Greek genius would have been left to latter-day archeological digs. This simplicity however was tainted with a duality, which, the successors of the prophet carried to a high art: they created unbelievable beauty in architecture and poetry; an unbelievable ferocity in warfare. The splendor of the Ottoman Empire outshone Christianity till the Renaissance.

Mohammed on the Minus Side.

He did not leave behind unequivocally strict instructions on how his Koran is to be interpreted, and left Islam open to factionalism. On top of it, he pulled heaven down to earth, as he promised sexual pleasures of heaven but then mixed it with bigoted fundamentalism on earth. The Islamic revival, which characterized the second half of the twentieth century, and is also burgeoning today, has missed history's train, and can only be regarded as anachronistic in the age of the split atom. Islam needs another prophet to heal the Sunni/Shiah schism. But even then, mankind could not build on Islam's metaphysical ideas, because they lack openness toward current, scientific cosmologies.

*   *   *

With this the prophets rest.

Closing Words

It is very likely that all religions can be characterized by saying that they are "approximately adequate" expressions of metaphysical views, for a segment of humanity, within a well-defined territory and a specific period of history. The longevity of religions does not contradict this statement, as, after their "zenith," they should be discounted as dynamic entities, to give room to a new metaphysics. I set out to determine what lasting values religions have left us with, and what "advanced" thoughts they did inspire, which could guide us towards that new elusive metaphysics, which I would call the secular and practical morality of this millennium. But, how to get there?

Is there a unified theory, which merges morality, metaphysics and mankind? Can I close this book with something of value? Or did I only make the question mark bigger?

Science has not succeeded yet in producing a unified concept between the general theory of relativity and quantum mechanics, though it deals with fantastically small units, units that are 10 mm/1,000,000/1,000,000 of magnitude. (Close to physical micro infinity?)

Philosophers have not succeeded either. If there was a unified metaphysical theory, then I probably would have my answers, and would not have to examine either the second alternative of my trilogy: "There is no god"; or the third alternative: "if there is no god, what is out there, and what is in here, in our hearts?"

Up to now the keepers of morality were the religions. But

they failed to go beyond fables, and insupportable, dogmatic "certainties"!

They concocted stories, sometimes beautiful stories, and expected their fellow men to believe them. When thinking about these stories, however, some of these men felt compelled to ask themselves about reality, and examine the feedback through their own critical faculties and from those of their contemporaries. When they did not get the answers they anticipated, or, when they did not get any answers at all, they had to face the possibility that they had to get the answers outside their current bounds, preferably in the physical-material world, where things appeared to be more readily solved than in the spiritual world. Secularization had begun and mankind penetrated deeper and deeper into the molecular world, probing the limits of miniaturization. Not even science has finished with the process yet. Imagine god!

We are still far from understanding physical micro infinity, and spiritual micro infinity is equally elusive. Do I know what they are? Do I talk nonsense? Perhaps, but, intriguing nonsense. (If you study the function of the "neurons" of the brain, you might agree with me that these ideas are not so far-fetched after all.)

With a dilettante's mind I have created these concepts, to arrive at a point, where even god may have to stop. Any comments my lord?

What you called "miniaturization" is indeed the road to the ultimate platform, where the divine will operates best. But, how small is really small? The figure you have quoted is no doubt approaching your "micro-infinities," i.e. the points, where, according to you, even I have to stop, though, if I am relative, then that point must be relative too, and, therefore, perhaps, I may not have to stop. (This "if" of course, is based on your "logic.") Now, how does this relate to your "prophets"? Of course, relatively. Relatively to their performance in regard to approaching that platform with their spirituality. Did they get any closer than their predecessors? I think they did, and that is the reason that I have been debat-

ing this point with you. Actually, you have demonstrated something like that, when you constructed your "evolutionary spiral," and indicated a degree of increased sophistication in your "actors," or a degree of totalitarian depravation in your modern-day, extremist "prophets." You were right to include Stalin and company in your examples, because they were driven by the same illogical zeal, as was used by the more dynamic individuals of your religious organizations. Both were experimenting (everyone is naturally) to determine how far they could push the human animal. The difference is that Stalinism lived only a century or so, while Hinduism, Buddhism, Christianity and Islam have shown considerable longevity, and tenacity. That communism did not survive longer would support the argument, that there must be something "positive" in your divine spark, which, sooner or later will gain the upper hand, by letting logic prevail.

The great experiment in the meantime will go on, and might produce even more aberrations. It is the strengthening of the basic morality of your species (which you advocate and with which I agree) that will pull you back from further futile efforts and attempts at what you call bringing about "social justice." The relentless inertia which you have created by building fear-governed religious systems is working against you. Mankind needs a little more courage, and just a little more selflessness, to turn things around, and to look at my world, and yours, logically. In looking at your selected, ancient prophets, you have not softened your attitude much, though you have acknowledged plus and minus qualities in them. Perhaps at this point we should agree to disagree and differ, and give a chance, and some time, to those, who, now, are in a position to change the course of your history, and develop your suggested, new morality. They should read your book.

Thank you, my Lord.

Can I start writing my second book in which you are **not?**

Yes! That will be fun, as you would say.

Appendix
The 21 Points of a 21st-Century Morality Code

(Assuming that there is a god)
(First draft)

1. Accept the Universe as a manifestation of an all-permeating life-force, of which you are a part. Being a part of it, act the part.
2. Accept that life-force, as being inseparable from an all-permeating intellect, and call the combination of the two, the god of creation.
3. Accept that this god has no image, no limit, but has an all-permeating presence, though relative in his powers regarding infinity.
4. Accept that this god is a god of logic, without feelings or emotions, though he is aware of both. Give this god due consideration.
5. Accept that this god's purpose is to experiment with the universe, including us, and that this experiment is still ongoing.
6. Accept that this god is so complex that he is beyond our full comprehension, yet so understanding and purposeful that we don't have to worship him. We can talk to him and he will answer.
7. Accept that this god has acknowledged kinship with us,

has given us his "divine spark" to get acquainted with him, has talked to us, and told us that we don't have to fear him.

8. Accept that this god is so superior to us that we don't have to love him, or hate him or deny him, but we can respect him for the beauty of this world.

9. Accept that it is acceptable to this god that we ourselves want to be gods as well, and that he supports our endeavor because the reason he has evolved/created us was to find out how far we can develop our divine spark, in the framework of his "great experiment."

10. Accept that due to our kinship with this god, via our divine spark, we also are bound to experiment, and explore our inner and outer universes for a thousand generations. And more.

11. Accept that it is you, and only you who can define this god's entity and that, therefore, you have to reject earlier definitions of this entity, as they only contain partial or distorted truths.

12. Accept that your makeup is the result of a long evolutionary process. This make-up is not dissimilar to that of the animal world and to maintain it you have to alternately act, rest, take food, and rest again. You do not lose by learning from the animal world. The divine spark of plants and animals is intuitive, rather than cognitive, but equally valuable.

13. Accept that your family, which is the basic unit of society, deserves respect and project that respect into the greater family of humanity. Appreciate sound traditions. Learn from the past.

14. Accept that life is precious, and is not resurrectable. Take life only when it is necessary for your sustenance, or for the protection of your family, or of yourself, or of your rightful possessions. Extend this rule universally

but do not shrink from controlled euthanasia. When god built obsolescence into us, he gave us the right to die.

15. Accept that for an orderly functioning of society, contractual obligations are necessary. Observe these obligations, and help others to fulfill them as well. Respect the law, but not uncritically. Improve the law continuously.

16. Accept that property and possessions are dear to the human heart and represent an enclave of security. Respect and protect that security.

17. Reject falsehoods and outdated axioms and teachings, which cannot be supported by scientific proof or historical, irrefutable evidence. Do not be sentimental in judging old books or traditions just because someone claimed that they contain the word of god, and do not be afraid to say: I don't know. Stop sometimes to reflect. Stop often to contemplate.

18. Reject the right of religions, sects and secret organizations to manipulate, monopolize or corrupt the spiritual life of individuals (especially the young ones), and reject the claim that these self-serving bodies have an exclusive commission to communicate with god. Always strive for the best attainable truth.

19. Do not be afraid of your sexuality. Your way to godhood is through your progeny. Enjoy all aspects of your life: your creativity, your work, your play, your spirituality and your sensuality. Plan your future and make sure that the next generation will be healthy and sane. Do not be afraid of selective breeding or genetic engineering. Nature will deal harshly with excessive overpopulation. And so will god.

20. Do not be afraid to learn selectively from the prophets. Emulate their spiritual strength and power of concentration and persuasion, despite their imperfections. Try to imitate the openness of Brahma; the serenity of Buddha;

the self-serving hard-line of Moses; the logic of Confucius, the ethics and courage of Zarathrustra; the compassion of Jesus; and the practicality of Mohammed, but believe in yourself and not in religion.

21. Do not stop marveling at the "miracle" of life, and continue searching into its reality. Aim for an inner balance and contentedness, and radiate happiness through your smile, especially towards the young. Do not be afraid to say: I love you. Continue assisting god in his great experiment, by doing your own increasingly complex experiments. Do not ever give up aiming for godhood. Talk to god. Cultivate your divine spark.

(Is it too simplistic? Try it!)
(You can even try to leave god out of it . . .)
But can we leave you out of anything? My Lord!)
DOMINUS VOBISCUM IN AETERNAM, AMEN.

THE DIVINE SPARK

THESAURUS

The spelling in this book is largely arbitrary, non-conformist, and non conventional.
It is meant to convey a "relative" importance of things, thoughts, and thespians.

A

absolute	perfect in quality or nature; ultimate
abstract	considered apart from concretums; theoretical
absurd	foolishly incongruous or unreasonable; ridiculous
ad nauseam	to a sickening or tedious degree
after life	a life believed to follow death
agnostic	someone who doubts the existence or knowability of god, but does not deny the possibility that god exists
Allah	the supreme being in the muslim religion; the god of islam
altruism	concern for the welfare of other human beings; selflessness
amoeba	a protozoa, a single cell microscopic organism
anachronism	out of and not in harmony with current time
animate	filled with life
animism	cultural belief in spiritual forces
antropomorphic	human like; made to resemble human characteristics
aphorism	a pithy statement of a truth, or opinion; a maxime; an adage
apogee	the highest or farthest point of an object
ascheticizm	the renouncing of material comforts for a life of austere self discipline
astral body	star-like; non-physical substance corresponding to the physical body
axiome	a self evident truth; a maxime; a fundamental principle
amino acids	essential components of protein
avatar	incarnation of or as, a deity; (Vishnu)

B

benevolence	a tendency to perform charitable acts; goodwill
Big Bang	the start of the universe by the explosion of a very dense mass
black hole	a star collapsed to such a dense mass that not even radiation can escape from it
Brahma	the absolute; the personification of the divine reality; prophet; part of hindu trinity
Buddha	indian mystic; prophet; founder of buddhism
buddhism	the doctrine that suffering is inseparable from existence, therefore inward extinction of the self and of worldly desires is needed to achieve Nirvana

C

caste	hindu, hereditary social class
category	division in a system; class
causal-interdependency	a relationship of cause and effect, in their mutual influence on one- another
charlatan	a person, who claims to possess knowledge or skill that he does not have; a quack
chosen people	the israelites, to receive god's revelation
century	a period of 100 years
cosmic resonance	the interaction of universal driving forces
cognitive	pertaining to the mental process, dealing with knowledge, perception and reasoning
conceptualize	to form theories, ideas
Confucius	chinese philospher; prophet; who emphasized personal virtue, devotion to family (ancestry) and justice
continuum	succession; continuous extent
cosmology	philosophy of the origin, process and structure of the universe
cosmogony	theory of the origin of the material universe; creation; genesis
cosmos	the universe as an orderly, harmonious whole
creation	god's primal act of bringing the world into existence
creator	god
crusades	military expedition to retake the holy land from the muslims

D

deification	to make a god of...; to glorify; to worship as a...
Dharma	the eternal law of the universe
dialectic - materialism	logical examination to determine validity; the doctrine of Marx/Engels
divine spark	spiritual heritage from god
doctrinaire	impractically, inflexibly theoretical; dogmatic
doctrine	accepted teachings of a religion, not based on proof
dogma	system unit of unfounded principles, beliefs
dogmatic	arrogantly authoritative of unproven tenets
duality	the state of being composed of two "principles"
dualism	the universe as made up of mind and matter; the juxtaposition of god and devils; good and evil
dubito ergo cogito, cogito ergo sum	I am doubting, therefore I am thinking; I am thinking, therefore I am (Descartes)

E

earth	fifth planet of the solar system
east	cardinal point of the compass, where the sun rises
ego	the self; the conscious aspect of the psyche
elite	the leading intellectuals, businessmen and politicians of a social group
elitist	professing or serving the superiority of the elite
emotion	a surge of strong feeling; mental agitation; sensory reaction to stimuli
epileptic	suffering of convulsion; conscious or un-conscious
escathology	doctrine of death, judgement, heaven and hell
eternity	endless and beginningless duration (time related infinity)
etymology	the study of words; their origin
eugenics	genetic engineering to improve a species
euthanasia	mercy killing
ex-cathedra	with authority; in an official capacity
exalted	made noble; raised in rank; honoured
existentialism	philosophy of the active role of the will rather than of reason in a hostile universe; an ethical philosophy of responsibility

F

fetish	an object regarded as having magic powers
force	power, or energy; anything that changes the "rest" or "in-motion" state of a body
free-radicals	an oxigen atom which is missing an electron and is constantly replaces it at the expense of another molecule; they are counter-acted with anti-oxidants
fundamentalism	the belief that all statements in the Bible, Koran, etc. are to be taken literally

G

galaxy	a large system of stars; e.g. the milky way
gene	protein molecule, transmitting hereditary characters by imprint
genetic	the interaction of genes
Genie	(Jinni) muslim supernatural being, serving man
genius	extraordinary intelligence, an outstanding mental gift
geocentric	with the earth as the centre of the universe
glasnost	change towards openness
globalization	international control of economy etc.
god	creator and ruler of the universe
godhead	the essential nature of god,; divinity
goodhood	the state of being divine
gospel	the teachings of the christian church; New Testament

H

hallucination	auditory, visual, or tactile perception; without external cause or stimulus
hegemony	domination; predominance; sole influence over land and people
hierarchy	rule by successive order or class of people, usually inherited; characteristic of theocracies
hinduism	brahmanism; the religion of hindus in India
homoiusion	transubstantiation; conversion of bread and wine into the body and blood of Jesus (Jesus is similar but not same with god) (Heterousion)
homousion	consubstantial (Jesus with god) (same); in eucharist: bread=body, blood=wine (the sameness of Jesus and god) (Nicaea)
humanism	study of classics; renaissance; emphasis not on religion but on human interest
huri	heavenly odalisque
hypnoses	trance-like condition; can be artificially induced, resulting in increased responsiveness to suggestion

I

idiom	special terminology, a dialect of meaning
image	a representation of the likeness of a person, creature, or object
immaculate	without stain, pure; ... conception=non sexual fertilization
impasse	deadlock; stop of progress
infinity	a state without end, beginning or limit; space related extent
inscruitable	incomprehensible; cannot be searched out
intelligence	the faculty of comprehending meaning; the ability to manipulate symbols
intransigence	a refusal to compromise, or come to terms
intuition	awareness of something without conscious reasoning, or sensory input
iota	the ninth letter in the greek alphabet; an insignificant amount; (see: homoiusion)
islam	the religion of muslims founded by Mohammed; mohammedanism

J

Jacob	(Isac's son) father of the 12 tribes of the hebrews
Jesus	jewish founder of the christian church; self styled messiah; prophet

K

Kaaba	muslim shrine in Mecca (a black meteorite)
Karma	the "feat" (act), by which you deserve your "fate"
kingdom	territory or state ruled by a king; a sovereign domain
kinship	relationship (mostly by blood)

L

laboratory	a place for scientific experimentation, research, testing
Lao-tse	chinese philosopher; founder of Taoism
lebensraum	territory, deemed to be necessary for a nation's economic wellbeing
legacy	something handed down from an ancestor, or from the past
lese-majeste	an offense, committed against a ruler, or supreme power; treason
limbo	an intermediate state of affairs (souls) etc.
locomotion	the ability to move from place to place
logic	the study of systematic reasoning; the opposite of irrational arguments
lord	man of high rank; a feudal magnate; god

M

macro	largeness in extent, duration, or size
man	a human; male or female; humanity
mantra	a sacred prayer formula which, when repeated, has magical powers
medium	a person thought to have powers of communication with the spirits of the dead
mesmeric	of hypnotic power
messiah	the anticipated deliverer and king of the jews
metaphysics	branch of philosophy which deals with the study of ontology and cosmology; i.e. the study of the "meta-ta-physica", things beyond the physical world
micro	smaller, more detailed
miniaturize	greatly reduce in size
modus operandi	a manner in which something works
Mohammed	founder of islam; prophet
molecule	simplest unit consisting of atoms and electrons, characteristic of a particular .matter
monad	undividable unit; basic constituent element of physical reality; (also spiritual)
monotheism	belief in one god
morality	correctness of character and behaviour
Moses	hebrew prophet, led the israelites out of Egypt; gave them the ten commandments
mudra	sacred gestures
mutation	heritable alteration of genes, or chromosomes of an organism
mysticism	spiritual discipline to access the divine by meditation
myth	traditional story

N

niche	a recessed, exclusive space for a statue or an idea
nihilism	a doctrine that denies existence; and all traditional values and institutions
Nirvana	extinction; the absolute happiness attained though the annihilation of the self
noetic	the regression of thoughts to their primeordeal base. where knowledge is obtained

O

obsolescence	the process of becoming useless
om mani padme hum	glory to the lotus (a mantra); the jewel is hidden in the lotus
omni	all
orectic	pertaining to desires; instincts
original sin	evil, inherent in man, because Adam ate the fruit of the forbidden tree of knowledge
Orwell	british writer; author of "1984"
Ottoman	turkish; muslim empire

P

panentheism	everything is god; immanently
panta rei	everything is flowing
pantheon	a gallery of gods
paradox	seemingly contradictory
parapsychical	telepathic; clairvoyant; dealing with the irrational
parsee	zoroastrian in western India
phalanster	a strictly organized social structure
pharao	king of ancient Egypt
pharisee	fundamentalist mosaic clergy
phenomenon	perceptible occurrance
philosopher	a student of intellectual enquiries
physics	science of matter and energy

P

pincer movement	military manoeuvre to encircle the enemy
pluralism	the world is a multitude of ordained, independent principles; not unified
pogrom	organized massacre; especially of jews
polarization	intrinsic separation of opposite poles, groups, opinions
polemic	argument; attack on an opinion, or doctrine
polytheism	belief in many gods
predestination	fore - ordaining of things, events
primeval	in the earliest age; ancient
primordial	existing in the beginning of time
pro-genesis	progeniture; begetting of offsprings
propensity	innate inclination
prophet	allegedly divinely inspired person; spokesman of a movement
pseudo	false, fake, or counterfeit
psyche	the soul, or spirit
psychology	the science to understand the mental process
psychopath	severe personality disorder

Q

quietism	passive contemplation
quintessential	purest or most typical
quo vadis domine	where are you going sir?
Quran	Koran; the sacred text of islam

R

reincarnation	rebirth into an other body
relativity	a theory of space, time and motion
religion	institutionalized system of belief
ritual	prescribed form of religious ceremony

S

salvation	the delivarance of men from the consequence of his sin
sanatana	eternal
sansara	the cyclic "panta rei" of the world
sanskrit	ancient, cultural, indo-european language
satire	a literary work of irony, caricature, and wit
schism	division into hostile fractions
schizophrenic	"split mind"; psychotic condition; withdrawal from reality
scriptures	sacred books
secularization	transformation from religious to civil influence
sex	a classification according to reproductive function
shaman	a primitive priest
shiah	minority sect of islam
Shiva	hindu god of destruction; part of hindu trinity
sine-qua-non	an essential element; condition
sophistication	to become more complex; refined
space-time	four dimensional continuum: three spatial one temporal
spirituality	an affinity to the metaphysical
sublimation	transformation of an impulse (e.g.sex) to a lesser behaviour pattern
sunni	majority sect of islam
sura	chapter of the Koran
symbol	a descriptive representation of an object or an idea
synthesize	to combine as to form a new complex product

T

tabula rasa	a clean slate; an opportunity to start anew
T'ai Ki	the ancient beginning
tao	the universal force that produces harmony in nature
tetrahedron	a polyhedron with four plane faces
theism	belief in a personal god, creator
theocentrical	centering on god as a prime mover
thesaurus	list of words; a specific dictionary

T

thespian	actor
tour-de-force	a feat of strength, or skill
transcendent	beyond human experience, or reason
travesty	grotesque representation
trepanation	skull perforation
trinity	three of something (father, son, holy ghost) (Brahma, Vishnu, Shiva)

U

uhr-alt	extremely ancient
universe	the whole of creation; the world

V

vedas	ancient hindu scriptures
virgin birth	birth without previous sexual intercourse
Vishnu	hindu god; prophet; part of hindu trinity

W

weltanschaung	world view
west	cardinal point of the compass where the sun sets
world	the universe; the earth; also symbolically
wu ki	the beginning, without a beginning

Y

yang (+) (sen)	male; positive; good
yin (-) (kui)	female; negative; evil
yoga	hindu system of meditation and excercise
yogi	a practitioner of yoga

Z

Zarathustra	founder of mazdaism; prophet (persian form)
Zoroaster	(greek form)
Zend Avesta	the sacred book of the zoroastrians
Zen	buddhist system of meditation
zenith	the highest point over an observer